THE CLASSIC WHEAT FOR MAN COOKBOOK

THE CLASSIC WHEAT FOR MAN COOKBOOK

More than 300 delicious and healthful ways to use stoneground whole wheat flour

Written and compiled by

VERNICE ROSENVALL,
MABEL H. MILLER,
DORA D. FLACK

Design and Illustrations by
Walt Woesner/Concerned Communications

WOODBRIDGE PRESS PUBLISHING COMPANY
Santa Barbara, California 93111

Published by
WOODBRIDGE PRESS PUBLISHING COMPANY
Post Office Box 6189
Santa Barbara, California 93111

By arrangement with
Bookcraft, Inc., Salt Lake City, Utah 84119

Original copyright © 1966 by Vernice G. Rosenvall,
   Mabel H. Miller, Dora D. Flack

This new edition
Copyright © 1975 by Woodbridge Press Publishing Company

All rights reserved.

World rights reserved. This book or any part thereof may not be reproduced in any form whatsoever, whether by graphic, visual, electronic, filming, microfilming, tape recording or any other means without the prior written permission of Woodbridge Press Publishing Company, except in the case of brief passages embodied in critical reviews and articles.

LIBRARY OF CONGRESS CATALOG CARD NUMBER: 75-17276
INTERNATIONAL STANDARD BOOK NUMBER: 0-912800-16-X

Published simultaneously in the United States and Canada

PRINTED IN THE UNITED STATES OF AMERICA

Preface

The authors' exciting "adventures in the wheat field" began in 1950. Like many of our associates, we had stored large quantities of wheat against a time of need. Now came the query, How shall we best prepare and use these golden kernels? So began our quest for knowledge and skill in the use of whole wheat.

Our first edition of *Wheat For Man* was published in 1952, when there was only limited help for an awakening interest in the "why" and "how" of wheat usage. Through a continuing process of trial and error, search and research, this present edition has evolved, containing more than three hundred choice recipes, each one carefully tested.

Over the years our book has been used internationally by countless thousands. Clearly, whole wheat cookery is gaining impetus and acceptance. This new, enlarged and revised edition includes information about a number of food discoveries made in connection with the use of wheat. Here are many new, delectable recipes, including a revolutionary, quick recipe for whole wheat bread.

It is our sincere hope that you will find this edition of *Wheat For Man* a valuable addition to your kitchen library.

Contents

PART I THE STAFF OF LIFE

Wheat, the Staff of Life	6
Houseware Helps	11
Baking Hints	12
Use Every Crumb	16
Sprouted Wheat	17
Wheat Storage	19

PART II KNOW YOUR INGREDIENTS

Honey	22
Dough Conditioner	24
Whey	25
Yeast	26
Baking Powder	28
Gluten Flour	29
Bread Enrichment	31

PART III RECIPES

Cereals	37
Bread and Rolls with Yeast	47
Quick Bread and Rolls	79
Meats, Casseroles	95
Vegetables	133
Soups, Sauces, Savories	139
Cookies	149
Cakes	175
Desserts	207
List of Recipes	226

PART I

THE STAFF OF LIFE

THE STAFF OF LIFE

Wheat, The Staff of Life

Wheat is one of the oldest and most basic foods of all time and has for centuries been regarded as the staff of life. It was cultivated from early times throughout the East, especially in Egypt. This country served as the granary of the Mediterranean area, notably in the Roman period when it shipped much of its wheat to Rome (Acts 27:6-38). In Palestine wheat grew in all the fertile valleys and plains. It was planted in December and harvested between April and June, the harvest season being observed as one of the year's festivals (Exod. 34:22). For human consumption, the kernels were either roasted (Ruth 2:14) or ground into flour for bread (Exod. 29:2).

There is scarcely any need to emphasize the importance of wheat to man's existence. Bread has made and unmade kingdoms and empires.

It is wisdom to prepare for a time when we might have to rely upon the resources of our own homes, in which case, because of its "whole food value," wheat should be the backbone of our storage program. Wise homemakers will therefore learn to use it.

Without getting into the technical aspects of flour milling, basically there are three methods of making flour from wheat:
1. *Roller milling*, which is used by large commercial flour mills in which the bran and germ are removed and the endosperm becomes silky, fine, white powder which is deposited into bags and hence to the supermarket for consumer use. Since most of the nutrients of the wheat kernel are removed in the process, a few synthetic vitamins and minerals are added to the flour and it is called "enriched flour." Bleach and sometimes preservatives are also added.

THE STAFF OF LIFE

2. *Burr milling*, which is accomplished by cutting the whole kernel. Burr milling produces the best cereals, but the flour is quite coarse. The resulting flour is rather heavy and tends to "drop" through the sifter.

3. *Stonegrinding* reduces the entire grain, bran, germ and all to a fine flour, generally by two stones rubbing the kernel which spreads the wheat germ evenly throughout the flour and there is no concentration of oil. At least one home mill has only one stone but the kernels are driven with great force against the stone to reduce them to flour. Stoneground flour should be fine and powdery and should therefore sift lightly through the sifter, insuring excellent baking qualities. If your mill does not produce this quality of flour, you should have it serviced.

Previously, commercial roller whole wheat flour was not suitable for the recipes in this book and most brands still fall into that category. In 1974, however, the top milling companies in the United States put on the supermarket shelves a whole wheat fine-textured flour which can bring excellent results when used in most of these recipes. But only *freshly ground* whole wheat flour insures full flavor and the maximum nutrition.

Introduce whole wheat products to your family gradually. They will adjust to the change and be grateful to you. Don't expect them to live entirely on wheat (although they could in case of an emergency). Strive for a balanced diet.

THE STAFF OF LIFE

As you become accustomed to whole wheat flour, you will gradually add other recipes to those in this book because you will find that stoneground whole wheat flour can usually be substituted successfully in practically any good recipe if the following simple rules are observed: When a recipe calls for 2 cups of *unsifted* flour, use 2 cups of *sifted* whole wheat flour; when the recipe requires 2 cups *sifted* flour, use 1 ¾ cups of *sifted* whole wheat flour.

One source of information on wheat, other food storage items, hand grinders and electric mills is Perma-Pak, 2457 South Main Street, Salt Lake City, Utah 84115. There are other reliable food storage outlets in many parts of the United States and abroad.

We heartily recommend that a hand grinder be in every home for cracking grain for cereal and for grinding coarse flour in case of power failure or other emergency. The hand-ground cereal can be used with white or whole wheat flour in making cracked wheat bread. However, *this flour should not be confused with stoneground flour which is required for the recipes in this book, because the flour is not as fine.*

Many good stonegrinding home mills are available. *Investigate, test and compare before purchasing*. We do not endorse any specific mill, but a few which we believe to be satisfactory are listed alphabetically below. Undoubtedly there are others available in different geographic locations.

All-Grain Mill, All-Grain Company, P.O. Box 168, Brigham City, Utah 84302 or 425 West Main, Tremonton, Utah 84337

Lee Mills, Lee Engineering Co., 2023 West Wisconsin Ave., Milwaukee, Wisconsin 53233

Magic Mill, 235 West 200 South, Salt Lake City, Utah 84101

Marathon Uni-Mill, Suncrest Products, Inc., Department #WFM, 2111 South Industrial Park Ave., Tempe, Arizona 85282. Toll free phone 800-528-1406

Mill 'n Mix, 3068 Highland Drive, Salt Lake City, Utah 84106. Handles most wheat grinders and mixers. Information available on all dealers and distributors throughout United States.

THE STAFF OF LIFE

The Miracle of a Wheat Kernel

The wheat kernel, broken down and analyzed, is found to consist of three important parts:

1. Bran, or outer covering, made up of layers rich in many vitamins and minerals as well as high-quality protein.

2. Germ, or embryo, from which springs new life. The wheat germ is one of the richest known sources of B and E vitamins and contains protein, fat and mineral matter. The germ and bran contain organic phosphates, which provide brain and nerve food. Calcium for bone and teeth is also supplied from these parts of the kernel.

3. Endosperm, the inner part of the wheat kernel, where cellulose, starch and gluten are abundant, but very little vitamin and mineral substance is present. White flour is made principally from the endosperm. In white flour about one-half of the fat is lost. The fat from a wheat kernel has a high food value, since it also contains unsaturated fatty acids.

It is clear that consumption of the balanced, complete kernel is necessary in order to receive the full value from wheat, especially "trace elements" so essential to human nutrition. On the trace elements there is still much to be learned.

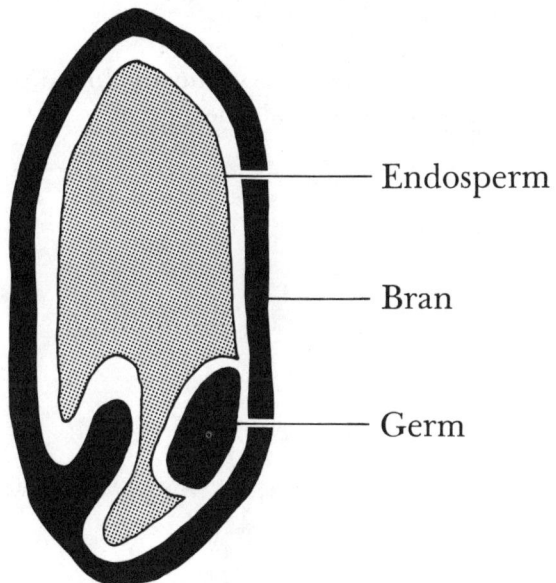

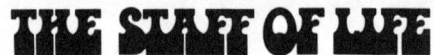

Known Minerals and Vitamins in a Wheat Kernel

Minerals:

calcium	flourine
iron	chlorine
phosphorous	sodium
magnesium	silicon
potassium	boron
manganese	barium
copper	silver
sulphur	and other trace minerals
iodine	

Vitamins:

vitamin A	niacin
vitamin C	pantothenic acid
thiamine B_1	inositol
riboflavin B_2 or G	folic acid
pyridoxine B_6	choline
biotin or H	plus others generally found in
vitamin E	bran and wheat germ

THE STAFF OF LIFE

Houseware Helps

Be proud of your role as a homemaker and take advantage of every kitchen aid on the market. The following equipment is considered essential to achieve optimum success from your baking efforts:

Mixing bowls with sloping sides
Ball-bearing rotary egg beater
Rubber spatula or scraper
Flexible metal spatula
Straight-edged knife for "leveling off" dry ingredients
Sharp knife for cutting refrigerator cookie dough
Measuring cups for dry ingredients ("measure line" even with top) —1 pint, 1 cup, ½ cup, ⅓ cup, ¼ cup
Measuring cup for liquids (with extra rim above "cup line")
Standard measuring spoons ¼ tsp., ½ tsp., 1 tsp., 1 tbsp.
Muffin tins
2 wire racks with legs to permit air circulation underneath
Rolling pin
Cookie sheets
Flour sifter
3 loaf tins, 9¼" x 4¾" x 2¾" (inside top measure) (2 lb.), or
5 Pyrex or metal loaf pans (1½ lb.) 8½" x 4½" x 2½"
Oblong pan, 8" x 12" x 2¼"
8" or 9" square pans
Layer cake pans, 8" or 9" diameter, 1½" deep
6-qt. pan for mixing bread (Dutch oven or deep well pan in range serves this purpose well)
Serrated sawtooth bread knife
2 or 3 large flexible paper plates with fluted 1" sides for sifting dry ingredients into
Bread board for kneading, or use table top. Canvas covered board is recommended.
Electric mixer
Blender

THE STAFF OF LIFE

Baking Hints

A soft dough makes better bread and rolls. This dough can be handled best by using a canvas-covered kneading board. Make a lightweight canvas cover to fit kneading board. (Cardboard may be used.) Measure length and width, allowing an extra 3-4 inches for shrinkage. Sew canvas on 3 sides, like a pillowcase, French seaming all raw edges to prevent fraying. Slip over breadboard and sprinkle lightly with flour for rolling, kneading or molding bread, rolls, pastry dough or rolled cookies. The canvas may be used several times between launderings if it is refrigerated in plastic bag after each use.

Powerful electric mixers are now available with various attachments: bread-kneading hook, juice extractor, lemon squeezer, cutting and shredding disc, grating attachment, mincer, noodle extruder, sausage filler and berry press.

The following hints may help you avoid disappointments and will make baking a pleasure.

1. Read entire recipe before starting to bake. Assemble all ingredients. Everything should be at room temperature, so remove them from refrigerator about an hour before using them. Preheat oven when you start mixing.
2. All measurements are level. Use standard measuring cups and spoons.
3. For everything except bread and some rolls, sift flour once before measuring, then twice with other dry ingredients.
4. Get acquainted with your oven. If it isn't baking satisfactorily, have it checked for correct temperature, or purchase an oven thermometer, which is available at small cost. If oven has a tendency to burn on the bottom, set baking pans on a sheet of aluminum foil or cookie sheet or any other large flat pan.

5. Freshness of all ingredients is absolutely necessary for good breadmaking. The oil in ground wheat can become rancid quickly and weevils may infest it. Whole grain flour, therefore, should be kept in a cool place if used within a week, and should be refrigerated if kept longer than a week. All flour can be frozen.

6. Wheat germ should always be refrigerated.

7. In stoneground whole wheat flour, *all* parts of the wheat kernel are present. Bran is nature's protective covering for wheat and is a naturally water-repellent substance; but the bran is desirable in food because of its rich mineral content. Bran must have a chance to absorb moisture in order that bread will not be dry and crumbly. Let dough stand at least three hours or, better still, overnight. With this method a more elastic dough results having better texture and more volume. Best results are obtained if the dough is kept as soft as possible—just stiff enough to handle.

8. The oven is a good place to set dough for rising, because there is no draft and it is usually warmer than elsewhere. Or better still, get the oven to a temperature of 80° or 85° simply by turning oven on for one minute. A gas oven with a pilot light is generally an ideal place for bread to rise because the oven is always warm. This "warming oven" method will cut rising time in half. If oven is in use, wet a doubled Turkish towel in very hot water, wring out and place over dough, or set bowl in a sink of very warm water, or place bowl on electric heating pad turned on "low."

9. If dough rises too much after shaping into loaves, it will fall, become coarse and open-grained and bread will be dry. If this happens, it is better to remold, even two or three times. A finer texture will result. The longer yeast is allowed to grow, the more the yeast plants multiply (tiny bubbles of carbon dioxide are liberated). Thus the texture of bread or rolls is finer. Therefore, whenever convenient, allow the dough to rise

THE STAFF OF LIFE

twice before baking. If time is not important, you can use less yeast but allow approximately half again as much rising time.

10. For a soft, tender bread crust, brush with butter or margarine and cover with towel while bread is still hot. For a crisp crust, do not grease—allow to cool uncovered. The cold loaves should be stored in plastic bags in a good bread box or, in hot weather, in refrigerator to preserve freshness, or freeze.

11. If you have a deep freeze, have a bread-baking day. Make at least twelve loaves. They will be just as good after having been frozen. For a small family, try slicing bread before freezing; wrap tightly to eliminate air; then remove a few slices as needed.

12. Raisin or date-nut bread can be made by adding a small amount of additional sugar, nuts and raisins or dates to one loaf of regular bread dough. This loaf will require more time for rising so always mold it first, then proceed to knead and shape the rest of dough for regular bread.

13. Large (46-oz.) juice cans, with one end neatly removed are fine for baking raisin-nut or date-nut bread. The round slices are different and attractive for luncheons or lunch boxes. When using cans and refrigerator roll dough, allow dough 1 hour and 15 minutes for rising. A double recipe for Refrigerator Rolls will make four cans. Drop the prepared dough into well-greased cans without pressing down. Cover can with foil and set upright in oven. Add 10 to 15 minutes to baking time when using cans instead of pans. Basic Bread recipe will make five cans.

14. When bread is baked, don't ruin the loaf by trying to cut it with a poor bread knife. A serrated sawtooth knife is ideal. To cut fresh, hot bread easily, heat the blade of the knife first, either in hot water or by holding it over electric or gas heat.

15. To reheat bread or rolls, preheat oven to 400°. Place bread or rolls in paper sack. Sprinkle sack with water. Turn off heat and place sack in oven for 10-15 minutes. With oven heat off, there is no danger of paper

THE STAFF OF LIFE

sack catching fire. Foil is also ideal. When using foil, preheat to 400°. Turn heat down to 200°. Let bread heat for 20-30 minutes, depending on size. To freshen stale bread or rolls, heat oven to 350°. Sprinkle bread with water. Wrap well in foil. Place in oven for 15-20 minutes.

16. For baking cakes, waxed paper cut to pan size to fit snugly in bottom of pan will insure easy removal of cake and will help to prevent burning. Alternatively, use waxed paper butter wrappers. Store wrappers in plastic sack in refrigerator for future use.

17. Don't "peek" at your baking until minimum baking time is up. Cake is done if it springs back when touched with fingertip. If impression of finger remains, it needs more baking time. When a cake comes from the oven, allow it to stand on cake rack for 5-10 minutes before removing from pan. This allows time for cell walls of cake to become set. Loosen sides of cake with spatula and out it comes—easy!

18. To keep cupcakes uniform in size, use a 1/4 cup measure to "spoon" batter into muffin tins.

19. Buttermilk and sour milk serve the same purpose and can be interchanged in recipes. Sour milk is obtained by adding one tablespoon of lemon juice or vinegar to a cup of fresh milk and letting it stand for a few minutes.

20. If raisins are to be ground, rinse them with hot water first—they'll glide through the food chopper with ease.

21. Raw sugar is available in all health food stores and any grocer can obtain it. Raw sugar has a tendency to become hard and lumpy. Store in tightly covered plastic containers or a bread box. If sugar becomes hard, place half a lemon or apple or potato in container with sugar and it will soften in a few hours; or put hardened raw sugar in the breadbox, where moisture from bread will soften it. Raw sugar is difficult to sift. Cream it into the butter, then add extract.

THE STAFF OF LIFE

Use Every Crumb

Salvage all stale bread, leftover toast or crusts and store in a cool, dry place. Keep soft crumbs in perforated plastic bag in refrigerator. Fine, hard breadcrumbs should be stored in covered jar in refrigerator or freezer.

In the event of a bread-baking failure, slice and dry the bread and make bread crumbs.

To make fine, hard bread crumbs, use bread that has been dried out in a warm oven or any dry, open place. Break one slice at a time into electric blender, or grind in food grinder, or place in plastic bag and crush with rolling pin.

Used in casseroles or gravies, bread crumbs act as thickeners.

Seasoned bread crumbs are excellent for coating meats, fish and poultry. Use seasonings of your choice, such as: paprika, pepper, parsley, onion salt, minced green onions, garlic salt, nutmeg, cinnamon, cloves, sage, oregano, etc.

Croquettes are easier to handle for baking and frying when rolled in crisp, seasoned bread crumbs.

Crumbs are a binder, filler, and extender when used in meat loaves, meat balls, etc.

Bread crumbs can replace part of flour in griddle cakes, cookies, and cakes, and will add to the lightness of the finished product.

As a topping for muffins, breakfast cakes, etc., try adding a few crisp crumbs to brown sugar, nuts and butter.

Note: For recipes using crumbs and stale bread, refer to sections: *Desserts; Meats and Casseroles, Sea Food; Vegetables; Soups, Sauces, and other Savories.*

THE STAFF OF LIFE

Sprouted Wheat

Sprouting seeds softens the tough outer coating of the kernel, making it more edible. The dry seed is also transformed into a living raw vegetable, containing a multiplicity of food nutrients.

Following is a very simple method for sprouting wheat:

Use cleaned, untreated, high-quality wheat. Divide 1 cup wheat into 2 one-quart wide-mouthed fruit jars or 1 one-gallon jar. Rinse well in several waters. Cover washed wheat with 2 cups room-temperature water. Place one thickness of nylon net, to act as a strainer, over opening of jar. Use heavy elastic band or fruit jar ring to hold net securely in place. (A piece of nylon stocking could be used in place of net.) After soaking for twelve hours, drain. Save water for drinking or cooking, since it contains some nutrients. Shake bottle to remove excess moisture. Place jar upside down and tip against edge of small sauce dish to allow for more drainage and air circulation. Place on countertop and cover with paper sack. Successful sprouting requires warmth, darkness, moisture and ventilation. Twice each day, morning and night, give the seeds a fresh-water rinse (room temperature) and return, tipped in the saucer.

Wheat should sprout 36 to 48 hours from beginning of soaking time, depending on room temperature. Sprouts are best when they are as long as the grain. Use immediately; growth can be retarded by storing in refrigerator. Never keep over one week.

WHEAT SPROUTS are delicious added to bread. *Method* 1. Put 2 cups of the recipe's liquid (see Basic Bread recipe) in food blender, set at *puree*. Add 2 cups sprouts gradually and blend thoroughly. Add this to the bread, as you begin with other ingredients. Rising action is somewhat slower. Bake about 10 minutes longer.

THE STAFF OF LIFE

Method 2. Grind 2 cups sprouted wheat, using fine disc. Knead into bread dough just before shaping into loaves. Method 2 is preferred.

Ground sprouts may be added to muffins, waffles, casseroles, meat loaf, etc. Whole sprouts may be added to fruit or vegetable salad, or may be eaten "as is."

Wheat Sprouts Candy

1 cup sprouted wheat
1 cup nuts
1 cup coconut
1 cup raisins, dates or figs
   or combination of these

Grind above ingredients in food grinder, using a fine disc. Mix well and shape into balls the size of marbles. Roll in fine coconut. Refrigerate.

Wheat Sprouts Meatballs

2 cups wheat sprouts
1 medium-size onion
1 cup nuts, optional
   (walnuts, pecans or almonds)
2 cups whole wheat bread crumbs
1 tsp. salt
2 tbsp. oil
1 cup milk
2 beaten eggs

Grind bread crumbs. Put sprouts, onion and nuts through food grinder, using fine disc. (Use one small piece of dry bread to force out all "nuts" in grinder.) Add salt, oil, milk and beaten eggs. Shape into balls about walnut size. Brown in oil in frying pan until golden brown and heated through.

If desired, serve with White Sauce (see recipe) to which parsley has been added before serving.

THE STAFF OF LIFE

Store Wheat Safely—
with these points in mind...

1. Choose dark hard winter wheat (turkey red) or dark hard spring or Marquis wheat. Insist upon grade No. 2 or better, weighing not less than 60 pounds per bushel, with at least 12 percent protein content. It should be cleaned and free from smut and foreign material, but *unwashed*.

2. Moisture content should be 10 percent or less. Insects are unable to reproduce in clean grain with a moisture content of 10 percent or below. Clean, fumigated wheat, hermetically sealed in cans, is available for storage. However, if you are placing untreated wheat in cans for storage, it is wise to take precautions to eliminate possible insect infestation which may not be visible. In circular No. 257 from the Utah State University, College of Agriculture, Extension Service, Logan, Utah, two treatments are suggested, either one of which is effective:

a. Spread two ounces of crushed dry ice over the bottom of the can and put the wheat immediately over the top of the dry ice. Allow sufficient time for the dry ice to evaporate before placing the lid on the can (approximately 30 minutes). Should pressure develop within the can (bulging) remove the lid cautiously, leave it off for about two minutes and then replace it. Follow this procedure in as dry an atmosphere as possible to reduce the condensation of moisture on the bottom of the can.

b. Place wheat in a shallow pan at a depth not greater than $3/4$ inches in an oven at a temperature of 150° for 20 minutes. Leave the oven door slightly open to prevent overheating. This treatment will destroy all stages of insect pests if the wheat is thoroughly heated. This same procedure may be followed if the wheat has too high a moisture content.

THE STAFF OF LIFE

3. Metal containers have proven to be most satisfactory for storage. Use containers that are not too large for convenient handling when moving is necessary. *Never* place metal containers directly on cement or dirt floors. Set them on wooden slats or shelves to prevent moisture from affecting the wheat or the container.

4. Quantity will vary according to individual needs. One year's requirement will vary from 70 pounds for a child to 300 pounds for an adult if circumstances should cause wheat to become the principal item of food. An active person would of course require more than an inactive one.

5. Wheat will keep indefinitely if properly stored in a cool, dry place with moisture content of wheat under 10 percent. The container should be placed so that it is free from any foreign materials, especially those which have odors, such as kerosene, onions, petroleum products, etc. If wheat is stored for more than one year, it should be turned and aerated at least twice a year (except in hermetically sealed cans). The most successful storage has resulted from rotation—using old wheat first and replacing it with new wheat at harvest season.

6. If wheat has already been thoroughly cleaned, no additional cleaning or washing is necessary before grinding. However, the following steps are suggested when cleaning is necessary:

a. Sieve to remove dust, grit, and other foreign materials.

b. Wash quickly three or four times in large pan, using ample water.

c. Spread out and dry thoroughly. If drying process needs to be hastened, place wheat in shallow pan at a depth not greater than ¾ inch, in an oven at 150° for 20 minutes.

d. Place the dry wheat in a container and grind as needed.

7. *Washed wheat should not be stored, as the moisture content is greatly increased with washing.*

PART II

KNOW YOUR INGREDIENTS

Know Your Ingredients

Honey

Color and flavor of honey varies with the type of flowers and plants the bees have visited. Darker honeys, which are produced in most parts of the country in late summer and fall, generally have a stronger taste and a higher mineral content. The darker varieties, like buckwheat and tulip poplar honeys, are preferred by most people for dark breads. The light honeys, which come from spring and early summer honey crops such as clover and alfalfa, are better suited to cookies, cakes, light breads, where the delicate flavor of the food might be overpowered by a strong-flavored honey.

Here are some suggestions for substitution of honey for sugar in recipes:

1. Use half as much honey as sugar called for in a recipe, or according to individual taste.

2. Honey is liquid, so slightly reduce liquids in the recipe or add a little more flour to get proper consistency.

3. Generally when honey is substituted for sugar in most baked products lower the oven temperature 25° to insure even baking inside and out.

4. Cakes, cookies and breads made with honey will be more moist than when sugar is used, and baked goods made with honey will keep longer without becoming stale. This is because honey is hydroscopic—it absorbs moisture from the air and holds the moisture in baked products.

KNOW YOUR INGREDIENTS

High quality, untreated, pure honey will eventually solidify or granulate. If new crop honey is purchased in large (60-lb.) cans, the fresh honey will probably be thick liquid. Immediately pour the honey into jars or small containers that can be tightly covered. Place these on the storage shelf for use one at a time. If honey is too thick or even solid, thinning it down will be desirable. CAUTION: Never overheat honey, or its delicate nutrients will be destroyed and honey will darken and change flavor. A small amount (½-1 cup) of too-thick liquid honey for immediate use can be thinned by putting it in a pan of hot water and leaving it at room temperature.

However, a quart jar or can of honey needs prolonged heating to liquefy it. Loosen lid of container and use a wire rack or hot pad on the bottom of a large pan partially filled with hot water instead of putting honey directly on the burner. NEVER PUT A CONTAINER OF HONEY DIRECTLY ON A BURNER. Keep the water at a temperature so that you can put your finger in and not have to pull it out immediately. If honey has been stored in plastic containers, extra precautions must be taken to prevent damage to the plastic bottom. Be sure to follow above instructions explicitly.

To keep honey from resolidifying, add 1 tbsp. water to each quart of honey, stir well. This should be done only as honey is brought from storage for kitchen use.

KNOW YOUR INGREDIENTS

Dough Conditioner

Dough conditioner is a very new, little-known product, which contains starch, salt, dextrose and an emulsifier. It helps baked goods to stay fresh longer, but is minus preservatives of any kind. Products made from whole wheat flour are naturally heavier than those made with white flour. Dough conditioner gives a lightness to any whole wheat baked goods—puts "spring" into it to keep it from being heavy.

4 oz. of dough conditioner would be sufficient for making 114 loaves of bread.

For bread: Add 1 tsp. dough conditioner to a small amount of the hot milk or hot water of bread calling for approximately 12 cups of flour. Cool slightly, then combine with dissolving yeast mixture and proceed according to standard instructions.

For cakes and cookies: Dissolve ½ tsp. dough conditioner in a little hot water for recipe which calls for 3 cups flour. Use less dough conditioner for a lesser amount of flour required in a recipe.

This unusual aid can be obtained from the manufacturer: Shirley J. Dough Conditioner, 766 Catalina Dr., Livermore, CA 94550

KNOW YOUR INGREDIENTS

Whey

What is it?

Whey (dried whey solids) is the goodness of milk after the cheese and butter have been removed. It contains many valuable protein components as well as vitamins and is 70 percent milk sugar, which is one-sixth as sweet as cane or beet sugar. The terms "whey" and "milk sugar" are used interchangeably. No salt has been added.

Whey is not a complete sugar substitute but reduces amount of sugar used in any recipe. When using whey, the end product will not be exactly the same as if only sugar were used.

Whey can be stored for an indefinite period of time in airtight, moisture-proof containers in a *cool, dry place*.

What does it do?

1. Aids in more attractive browning.
2. Relaxes dough for better texture.
3. Substitutes for a part of sugar in baked goods, desserts, drinks and even some candies.
4. Can be used as a milk extender: 1 part whey to 7 parts water and mixed with whole milk for greater nutrition and economy. Experiment a bit to suit the taste of your family.
5. Enriches all recipes with 12 percent more protein, vitamins and valuable minerals.

A very small recipe and fact booklet, *A Better Whey to Fine Cooking*, is available from Cache Valley Cheese, Smithfield, Utah, which is one source of supply. Perhaps there is a source of supply near you where you can obtain specific help.

One recipe in this book using whey is Superior Quick Whole Wheat Bread.

KNOW YOUR INGREDIENTS

Yeast

These are equivalent and may be used interchangeably: 1 tbsp. active dry yeast, 1 pkg. active dry yeast, 1 compressed yeast cake.

The yeast bread and roll recipes in this book call for a specified number of "tbsp. of yeast." Choose carefully your own type of yeast. The following information will assist in that selection.

1. Dried yeast granules in 2-lb. hermetically sealed cans, labeled "Active dry yeast for bakers," may be obtained from some supermarkets or from your bakery, and will "keep" in cool, dry storage for six months to one year. Whenever possible refrigerate or freeze it. When the can is opened, divide it into smaller containers which can be tightly covered. Keep one in the refrigerator for immediate use and the others on the storage shelf, *clearly marked for rotation,* if refrigerator space is limited. This 2-lb. can equals 128 tablespoons or envelopes of yeast or the equivalent of 128 yeast cakes. Compare this for economy. Smaller economy-size containers of yeast are also available in 4-oz. jars which contain the equivalent of 16 envelopes, or 16 tablespoons of yeast.

2. "Active dry yeast" (granular) in $1/4$ oz. tinfoil packets is the expensive route. Be sure to read the date lines on the container or label. Also determine whether BHA has been added. BHA is an abbreviation for butylated hydroxyanisole. BHT is an abbreviation for butylated hydroxytoluene. These two preservatives are anti-oxidants used to insure a longer shelf life.

3. "Instant blend yeast" ($1/4$-oz. package) is very small granules and does not have to be dissolved in water separately before being added to other ingredients, as is the case with other types of yeast, either dry or compressed.

KNOW YOUR INGREDIENTS

4. Good compressed yeast is grayish in color. It is brittle and crumbles easily when broken between the fingers. Compressed yeast can be purchased in some supermarkets in a .6-oz. cake, which equals one tablespoon of active dry yeast. But it is also available in bulk "bricks" of one pound at your bakery or most health food stores, resulting in great economy for the person who bakes a great deal. Compressed yeast is perishable and requires refrigeration. It will "keep" about two weeks. Freezing, for storage, is not recommended, but some homemakers have been successful at it. They divide the brick into equal portions the size of a .6-oz. yeast cake so that these can be thawed and used individually as needed. Be sure to let the yeast thaw in the refrigerator and not at room temperature. Experiment at your own risk.

Active dry yeast works best when dissolved first in warm water, 110° to 115°. At this temperature, water feels quite warm when dropped on the wrist. If possible, use a candy thermometer until you are able to recognize the correct temperature, because yeast will not activate if water is too cool, and a higher temperature may kill the yeast. Sprinkle yeast into the water and allow it to activate without stirring. A little added sweetening speeds activation. If yeast doesn't begin to bubble within twenty minutes, it may be dead. Try adding a pinch of ginger to rejuvenate it.

Know Your Ingredients

Baking Powder

There are three types of baking powder:
1. Double-action (Calumet, Clabber Girl, Davis, etc.)
2. Phosphate (Rumford, Dr. Price, etc.)
3. Tartrate (Royal, etc)

In most recipes, double-action baking powder is used. If you find it necessary to adjust your recipe for the kind of baking powder you use, this is the rule to follow. A given recipe would call for either 2 tsp. of type 1 (double action) or 2½ tsp. of type 2 (Phosphate) or 3 tsp. of type 3 (Tartrate). If you want to use Royal Baking Powder, for example, and the original recipe calls for 2 tsp. double-action baking powder, you will get better results if you increase baking powder to 3 tsp. Remember, too, that Royal Baking Powder is not double acting so it is important to get your product into the oven as soon as mixed.

Royal Baking Powder is made from cream of tartar, which comes from grapes, while many other baking powders are made from sodium aluminum phosphate.

The recipes in this book are developed for double-action baking powder because it is commonly used. Follow above instructions for adjusting.

KNOW YOUR INGREDIENTS

Gluten Flour

Gluten flour can be used advantageously in making bread and rolls, because it improves volume and elasticity. *Making this flour takes a lot of time and work.* If you have a convenient source of supply, buy the gluten flour instead of making it. Be sure to compare prices, since they vary in different health food stores. Buying in quantity, such as 5 or 10 pounds, saves money. However, if it is not available, the extra work is worth the results in better bread. This is especially true when the wheat being used for flour is not of high quality. Gluten flour greatly improves baking results from wheat of low—or undetermined—protein content.

In order to produce gluten flour, first make raw gluten which can be done by hand or in an electric dough mixer. When making by hand, use the basic amounts given below and knead thoroughly a good 10 minutes, pounding and rolling dough also to develop the gluten completely. Then follow all the other instructions outlined below after the words *"take out the dough hook."*

Electric dough mixer method:

    9 cups cold water in mixer bowl
    18 cups fine whole wheat stoneground flour

To the water in mixer bowl, add 6 cups flour, beating until well-blended. Then add another 6 cups. The last six cups must be sprinkled in slowly because of stiffness. Moisture content will vary with different wheat. Be careful that dough doesn't clean the bowl as in breadmaking. If it reaches that point, add a little water to restore moisture. Knead 5 to 10 minutes. Remove bowl from its base and *take out the dough hook.*

Completely cover gluten dough with water and let soak at least 2 hours or overnight, according to your own time schedule. This soaking results in a much greater yield of gluten flour.

KNOW YOUR INGREDIENTS

After soaking, with hands clean it away from sides and bottom of bowl. Pour first starch water off into another pan. Save water from gluten-making because it contains vitamins and minerals. Use it for breadmaking, mixing dry milk, gravies, soups, sauces, eggnog, banana drink, frozen fruit ices, etc.

Set colander with many small holes in pan of water. Add about 2 cups of dough at a time to colander, squeezing dough and pulling it away from the holes. It will seem to come apart and you think you'll lose it. Then suddenly it will act like bubble gum. Pick it up with both hands and, in a second pan, squeeze it under the cleaner water until the sandy feeling is gone and water runs clear. Set it aside and let rest in another colander at least a half hour to drain off as much moisture as possible.

Place raw gluten on lightly oiled cookie sheet or 2 or 3 bread pans. Push from the center out and stretch until it is fairly even, ½" thick. Bake 15 minutes in preheated oven at 350°. Twist fork in bubbles and thickly-raised areas to let out steam. Cook another 15 minutes or until it springs back when pressed.

Remove from oven and, if gluten seems crisp on top or bottom, either put it in a plastic bag or fold the large sheet of gluten until the steam adjusts the texture evenly, or sprinkle water on it. When there are no crisp areas, run it through the meatgrinder on medium disk, or grate on largest holes of a shredder. It will be soft and pliable.

Spread ground gluten on 2 cookie sheets. Bake at 200°, leaving oven door ajar until ground gluten is completely dry. Grind dry gluten granules in electric stonegrinder. This amount yields about 1½ pounds of gluten flour, or approximately 3 cups.

As an extra safety precaution for the mill, grind equal amounts of dried gluten granules with wheat. In so doing, remember—if recipe calls for ½ cup gluten flour, use 1 cup of the gluten-wheat flour mixture, then reduce by ½ cup the amount of flour called for in the recipe.

KNOW YOUR INGREDIENTS

Bread Enrichment

You can bake your own enriched bread by using natural additives to increase the nutritional qualities. Use your own judgment on how much of these additives to use. Some of them have distinct flavors of their own, hence some experimentation for your own taste preferences will be necessary.

Kelp—source of iodine
Brewer's yeast—source of B vitamins and protein
Wheat germ—source of vitamin E
Rice polishings—source of thiamine
Bone meal powder—source of calcium
Soy flour, grits and powder—source of proteins, vitamins; especially B vitamins
Peanut flour—source of protein, B vitamins and iron
Powdered milk—source of calcium. If using non-fat, it must be combined with oil or butter in the same recipe.
Sunflower seed meal—source of proteins, vitamins, trace minerals
Pumpkin seed meal—protein, iron and other trace minerals in the same recipe.

KNOW YOUR INGREDIENTS

Equivalents

a pinch or dash = less than 1/8 tsp.
3 tsp. = 1 tbsp.
2 tbsp. = 1/8 cup
4 tbsp. = 1/4 cup
5 tbsp. plus 1 tsp. = 1/3 cup
8 tbsp. = 1/2 cup
12 tbsp. = 3/4 cup
16 tbsp. = 1 cup
1 liquid ounce = 2 tbsp.
1/2 pint = 1 cup
1 pint = 2 cups
2 pints = 1 quart
4 cups = 1 quart
4 quarts = 1 gallon
8 quarts = 1 peck
4 pecks = 1 bushel
16 ounces = 1 pound
16 liquid ounces = 2 cups
28 grams = 1 ounce
454 grams = 1 pound
4 cups flour = 1 pound
1 cup white flour = 7/8 cup stoneground whole wheat flour
2 cups granulated sugar = 1 pound
2 3/4 cups brown sugar = 1 pound
1 cup granulated sugar = 1 cup brown sugar or 1 cup raw sugar (not so sweet)
1 cup molasses = 13 ounces
5 large eggs = 1 cup
8 egg whites = 1 cup
16 egg yolks = 1 cup
2 cups butter = 1 pound
4 cups grated cheese = 1 pound
2 cups ground meat = 1 pound
1 cup uncooked rice = 2 cups cooked
1 cup uncooked macaroni = 2 cups cooked
1 cup uncooked noodles = 1 1/4 cups cooked
1 large lemon = 1/4 cup juice
1 medium orange = 1/2 cup juice
2 cups dates = 1 pound
3 cups dried apricots = 1 pound
2 1/2 cups prunes = 1 pound
2 1/2 cups raisins = 1 pound
1 1/2 pounds apples = 1 quart
3 large bananas = 1 pound
1 cup nut meats = 5 ounces
1 pound potatoes = 4 medium-sized potatoes
1 pound tomatoes = 3 medium-sized tomatoes
1 egg is equal in leavening power to 1/2 tsp. baking powder

KNOW YOUR INGREDIENTS

Kitchen Math With Metric Tables

Measure	*Equivalent*	*Metric (ML)*
1 tablespoon	3 teaspoons	14.8 milliliters
2 tablespoons	1 ounce	29.6 milliliters
1 jigger	1½ ounces	44.4 milliliters
¼ cup	4 tablespoons	59.2 milliliters
⅓ cup	5 tablespoons, plus 1 teaspoon	78.9 milliliters
½ cup	8 tablespoons	118.4 milliliters
1 cup	16 tablespoons	236.8 milliliters
1 pint	2 cups	473.6 milliliters
1 quart	4 cups	947.2 milliliters
1 liter	4 cups, plus 3⅓ tablespoons	1,000.0 milliliters
1 ounce (dry)	2 tablespoons	28.35 grams
1 pound	16 ounces	453.59 grams
2.21 pounds	35.3 ounces	1.00 kilogram

PART III

RECIPES

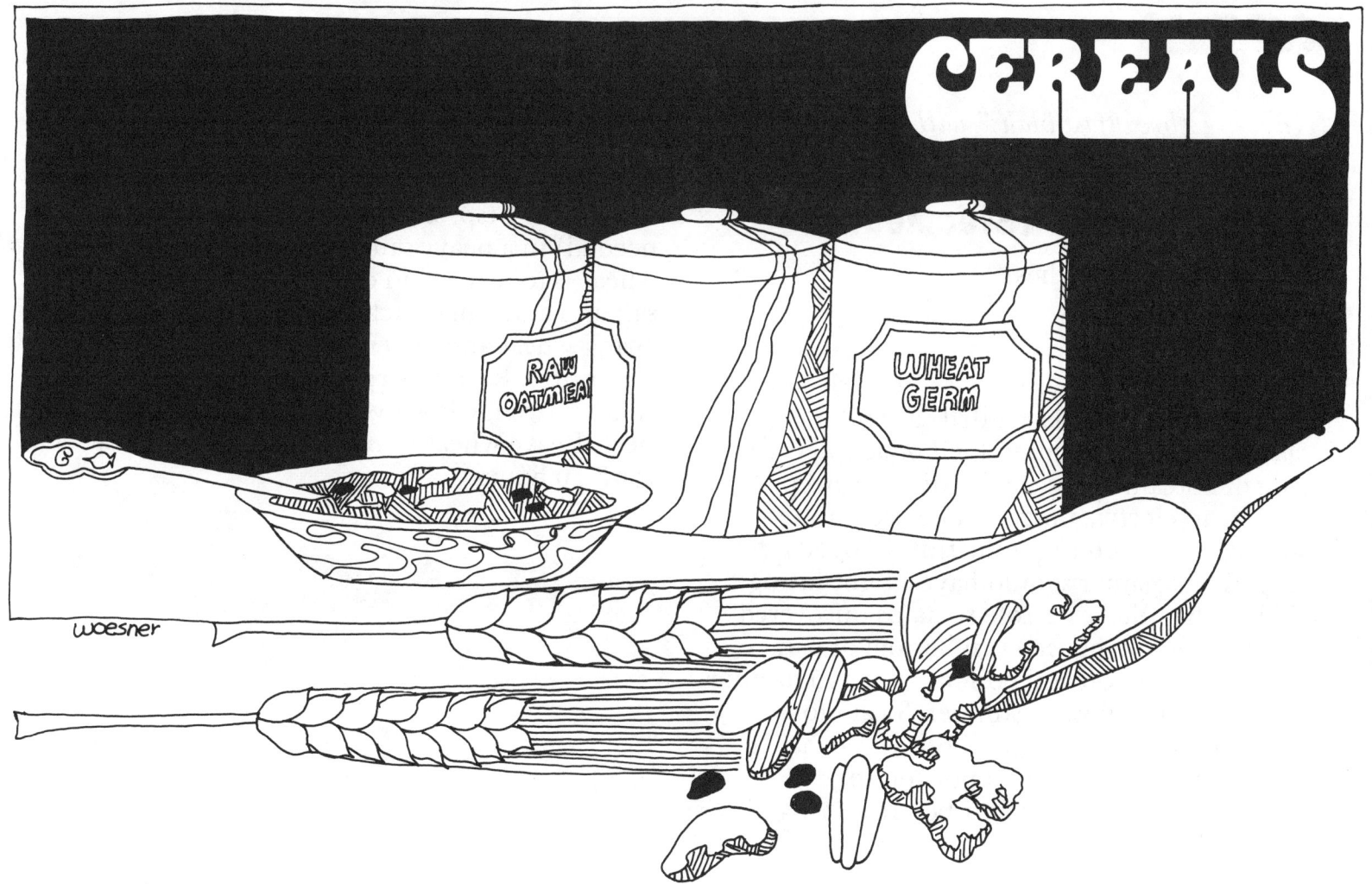

CEREALS

No more "breakfast blahs" with all this variety. The better the grain, the better the cereal.

Whole Wheat (Steamed)

1 cup clean whole wheat
1 tsp. salt
2 cups water

Place all ingredients in a casserole dish (1-or 2-quart capacity). Place filled casserole, *without a lid,* on a raised shelf or adapter ring of a steamer or deep kettle. The deep well in an electric range can be used. Fill steamer with water up to within 1" of adapter ring. The steamer should have a tight-fitting lid but the filled casserole remains uncovered all the time. Bring water in bottom of pan to full rolling boil and boil for about 15 minutes. Reduce heat to low or simmer. Steam for 10-12 hours or overnight. This recipe makes 10 servings. Keep unused portion in refrigerator and reheat just before serving.

Whole Wheat (Oven Cooked)

For cereal combine 2 cups water to 1 cup wheat and 1 tsp. salt (multiply amounts as needed) in a heavy saucepan. If whole-cooked wheat is to be used in other recipes, omit salt and add when included in another recipe. Bring wheat and water to a boil and cook 5 minutes. Remove from heat, cover and set in 300° oven. Close oven door and turn off heat. Leave wheat undisturbed overnight or for 8-10 hours.

Whole Wheat (Crockpot)

2 cups clean whole wheat
1½ tsp. salt
4 cups water

Place all ingredients in crockpot of 3- to 3½-quart capacity. Cover and cook on low heat 8-9 hours. If possible, stir once during first hour of cooking. This recipe makes 20 servings. Refrigerate unused portion and reheat just before serving. This cooked wheat may also be used in many bread and casserole recipes.

Whole Wheat (Thermos)

1 cup clean whole wheat
1 tsp. salt (optional)
2 cups boiling water

Boil wheat in water 3 minutes. Preheat thermos by rinsing with boiling water. Pour in boiling wheat mixture. Seal tightly and let stand overnight. It is then ready for morning cereal. Add honey, milk, dates or raisins as desired.

Canned Wheat

In some areas canned whole wheat is now available, which has many advantages both for storage and for daily use. As a cereal it can be heated (preferably in a double boiler) or, in an emergency, it can be eaten cold.

Added to many bread, roll, cake or cookie recipes, it not only adds extra food value, but gives a sweet, nutlike flavor and crunchy texture. It is also an excellent extender when used in meat loaves, meat balls or casserole dishes. It can also be added to some salads, stuffings and even candies. Try serving this wheat topped with gravy as a substitute for potatoes. Whenever cooked whole wheat is required in a recipe, canned wheat may be used.

CEREALS

Cracked Wheat Cereal

1 cup cracked wheat
4 cups water
1 tsp. salt

Method 1. Cook over direct heat about 30 minutes, reducing water to 3 cups, if desired; stir frequently.

Method 2. Cook in double boiler for 1 hour or more.

Method 3. Start in double boiler at night and cook 30-60 minutes. Let stand until morning, then cook at least 30 minutes longer.

Variations:

    Instead of using water, cook cereal in fresh milk or reconstituted powdered milk.

    Sprinkle toasted wheat germ on top of each serving (recipe below).

    Leftover cracked wheat cereal can be used in cracked wheat pudding in the Dessert Section.

Leftover cracked wheat cereal can be stored in the refrigerator in a straight-wall container. Chill, turn out and slice and fry in oil. Serve with butter and honey.

Cracked Wheat (Crockpot)

1 cup cracked wheat
1 tsp. salt
3 cups water

Cook in crockpot on high for 30 minutes. Turn to "off." Let stand overnight in crockpot. In the morning, turn heat on for 20 minutes or more, if necessary.

Gruel

2 cups water
½ tsp salt
⅓ cup cracked wheat

Simmer at least 45 minutes. Strain. Add 1 tsp. honey, dash of nutmeg, ⅓ cup canned milk or 2 tbsp. powdered milk. This makes 1 big glass. A larger amount of cracked wheat can be cooked and then refrigerated for later serving. This is excellent for ill persons or babies.

Whole Wheat Flour Cereal

⅔ cup whole wheat flour
2½ cups boiling water
½ tsp. salt

Mix flour, boiling water and salt, using a good eggbeater. Cook in double boiler at least 20 minutes or until thick.

If desired, add ¼ cup nuts or ½ cup raisins, dates or figs.

Serve with butter or cream. Raw sugar or honey may be used, if desired. This is suitable for babies or ill elderly people.

CEREALS

Toasted Wheat Germ

4 cups fresh wheat germ
½ cup warmed honey

Mix thoroughly. Spread mixture in a loaf pan or in small cookie sheet with sides. Toast 10 minutes at 300°. Cool. Pour into plastic bag or bottle and keep refrigerated. Serve as a cold cereal if desired with milk, or mix with any cold prepared whole grain cereal, or sprinkle on top of any cooked cereal. If natural flavor of wheat germ is enjoyed, omit the honey, but toast the same way.

Variations:

    Mix together ¼ cup wheat germ, enough cream to moisten, a grated unpeeled apple, 1 tsp. lemon juice and honey to taste.

    Add a few chopped walnuts.

Chewy Cold Cereal

10 shredded wheat biscuits, crumbled (Sunshine brand)
2 cups raw oatmeal
1 cup sunflower seeds, hulled
1 cup sesame seeds
½ cup wheat germ
½ cup powdered milk
½ cup rice polishings
½ cup raw or brown sugar
½ cup soya lecithin granules

Mix all together. Store in refrigerator. Serve with cold milk and raisins or other fruit, if desired.

Wheatnuts (Similar to Grapenuts)

3 cups coarsely-ground whole wheat flour
½ cup wheat germ
2 tbsp. malted milk powder, natural flavored, optional but very good
2 tsp. baking powder
½ tsp. salt
1 cup brown sugar
1 cup sour milk or buttermilk

Combine all ingredients. Stir well with a spoon. Dough will be very sticky. Pour onto greased cookie sheet, pressing to ½" thickness with a spoon. Pan will not be filled to edges. Bake at 350° 30-35 minutes or until firm but not crisp. *Turn off oven*. Remove pan from oven. Cut into strips 1" x 2". Turn upside down with a spatula on the pan and return to warm oven until *dried out thoroughly*.

Grind in food chopper, using coarse disk. Through a wire strainer separate the coarse from the fine crumbs. Use the coarse part for cereal and the fine part for cracker crumbs in desserts, especially graham cracker pie crust. Refrigerate unused amounts. Yields almost 1 quart cereal and almost 1 pint crumbs.

CEREALS

Granola Cereal

5 cups old-fashioned rolled oats or rolled wheat or rolled triticale (or combination of any of them)
1 cup sesame seeds
1 cup coconut
1 cup sunflower seeds
1 cup chopped almonds or peanuts
1 cup noninstant powdered milk
1 cup whole wheat flour
1 cup wheat germ
1 cup oil
1 cup honey
1 cup water

In mixer, combine oil, honey and water. Add dry ingredients. Beat until thoroughly mixed. Spread on 2 cookie sheets. Bake 45 minutes at 275°. Stir occasionally while baking. Add raisins, banana flakes, chopped dates, apple flakes or other dried fruits after baked, if desired.

Bulgur Wheat

If you have eaten in Armenian restaurants, you may have been served a delicious food made from precooked and dried wheat called bulgor or bulgur. Bulgur wheat has been a staple in the diets of the peoples of the Middle East for many centuries. When used in a variety of dishes, bulgur has the advantages of cooking more rapidly than whole or cracked wheat. Although commercially prepared bulgur is available, you may enjoy preparing your own.

CEREALS

To Make Bulgur Wheat:

In heavy saucepan, combine 1 cup wheat with 1 cup water. Cover pan and bring to a boil. Turn down heat and simmer 1 hour. Drain off any remaining liquid. Spread wheat in thin layer on large baking sheet and bake 2 hours at 200° or until wheat is completely dried. Leave oven door ajar slightly for moisture to escape.

Crack bulgur wheat in mill or grinder. In some recipes this may be used whole, giving a very chewy product.

This processed bulgur is easily stored in a dry, cool place and may be used in many recipes. However, we suggest it be used as fresh as possible for maximum nutritional value. If the recipe calls for cooked bulgur, simply boil in water 5-10 minutes. It will approximately double in volume.

If bulgur is not available or you do not care to make it yourself, substitute regular cracked wheat in most recipes.

Try serving bulgur wheat with a protein and vegetable plate. It has a sweet, nutlike flavor and crunchy texture. Bulgur wheat makes an excellent extender when used in loaves, Swedish meatballs, Mexican bulgur chili, or curry recipes.

Cooked and chilled bulgur may be added to your favorite cole slaw recipe for a most interesting and enjoyable salad.

Bulgur, soaked overnight in water, may be added to bread or yeast rolls for a nutlike flavor and texture. It can also be added to cookies. You will find recipes in Meats and Casseroles section calling for bulgur, or in which bulgur can be substituted for cracked wheat.

For further information and recipes, write to Western Regional Research Laboratory. Albany, California.

BREAD AND ROLLS~YEAST

Be sure to first read Baking Hints and Know Your Ingredients

General Suggestions for Making Bread

Remember—the better the wheat, the better the baking results.

One cup wheat makes 1½ cups flour.

Before measuring flour, it is a good idea to "lighten" it by stirring flour in the bag, thus insuring more accurate measurements. Freshly milled flour is airy and requires a little more in most recipes than "settled down" flour.

A soft, pliable dough gives better results. *Whole wheat flour* varies according to the protein and moisture content. In making bread and rolls, use the amount of liquid called for and the minimum amount of flour specified, then add more flour as needed for a soft dough. Dough that is too stiff produces dry, crumbly, coarse-textured bread. You will soon learn what is the right "feel" for perfect dough for your altitude and humidity.

In high altitudes over 4,000 feet, tested bread recipes require less yeast, a little more liquid and more and shorter rising periods, because dough rises faster in high altitudes. Punching down the dough at more frequent intervals keeps it from getting so light that the cell walls will be stretched too far. Also higher altitudes require a slightly higher baking temperature.

There may be times when you will want to use more yeast to speed up the breadmaking process. More yeast will hasten the rising periods, *but* the quality of the bread will not be as good. Both flavor and texture are improved when the fermentation is long enough for the desirable changes to take place in the gluten. A larger quantity of yeast in any recipe speeds rising; a smaller amount slows rising. Increased amounts of yeast do not cause a yeasty taste. But if the bread rises where temperature is too high, a yeasty taste results.

BREAD AND ROLLS~YEAST

When bread is done, it will shrink slightly from sides of the pan and sound hollow when thumped.

A perfect-shaped loaf of bread measures about the same in width and height. The crust should be thin, crisp and tender.

When using raw milk instead of pasteurized, heat to simmering to destroy molds and some bacteria which may affect the flavor of bread. Then cool to lukewarm (110° to 115°) before adding yeast.

When adding wheat germ to dough, if bread is not being baked within three hours, the wheat germ should be toasted for ten minutes at 300° or simmered in milk before being added to dough. Otherwise "runny" dough may result.

Thorough kneading is essential as it brings together the particles of gluten, resulting in elasticity, good texture and volume. Use a canvas-covered board, as explained in Houseware Helps.

Milk makes a more nutritious, bland product, but water permits a more pronounced whole-grain flavor. Potato water produces a more moist bread. A beaten egg promotes a lighter-textured bread.

To include soy flour, freeze soybeans and mix with wheat, grinding them together. Use 2 cups of this mixture in place of 2 cups straight whole wheat flour. If soybeans are ground in the mill alone and unfrozen, they will gum up the stones because they contain a large amount of oil.

One advantage of adding gluten flour, as in Superior Quick Whole Wheat Bread, is that volume is increased. For example, in a bread recipe normally yielding four loaves baked in 8½" x 4½" x 2½" loaf pans, you will now have five loaves that size. In a bread

BREAD AND ROLLS~YEAST

recipe normally yielding three loaves baked in 9¼" x 4¾" x 2¾" pans you will now have four loaves that size.

A bonus of the Superior Quick Whole Wheat Bread recipe is that excellent rolls can be made from the same recipe. Reserve one loaf portion and make 12-18 dinner rolls (depending on size) formed in any shape, such as hamburger or hot dog buns, Parker House rolls, etc. Hamburger and hotdog buns made from this recipe are superior to those made with the Refrigerator Roll recipe.

Pan size is extremely important—use pans not larger than 9¼" x 4¾" x 2¾" inside top measure. Pyrex loaf pans 8½" x 4½" x 2½" are excellent—lower the baking temperature 25°, since Pyrex retains more heat than metal. A metal pan this size is also available. Basic Bread recipe makes four loaves this size. Using narrow rather than wide, "squatty" pans insures a better-shaped and better baked loaf.

Glass, darkened metal or dull-finished aluminum pans produce a good brown crust. To darken the shine, place ungreased pan in 425° oven 4-5 hours. Alternatively, place pan in a cold oven, heat to 450°, turn off heat, then leave pan in oven until oven cools.

BREAD AND ROLLS~YEAST

If oven temperature is uneven, a large crack—called a *shell crack*—may develop on the cooler side of the loaf. This results from imperfect circulation around each loaf, caused either by a faulty oven or by crowding the loaves. At least 1 inch of space should separate the loaf pans.

If bread dough gets too light before the oven heat sets the cell walls, a *shell top* may develop. A slight jar can cause the light dough to fall either before or after the loaf goes into the oven, and although the baked loaf may look normal, the collapsing dough may have left a large hole under the crust.

Molding a Perfect Loaf of Bread

1. Press or roll each loaf separately into flat, oblong sheet.
2. From long side, fold $\frac{1}{3}$ of dough over and press to seal.
3. Fold other long side, overlapping first. Press and seal.
4. From end, fold $\frac{1}{3}$ of dough over. Press and seal.
5. Fold other end, overlapping the first. Press again. This vigorous pressure on each loaf removes air from dough and produces smooth, even-textured bread that is light without having large airholes.
6. Roll sheet of dough lengthwise, like a jelly roll, making a round, compact loaf. Seal overlap.
7. Place in greased loaf pan with overlap underneath.

BREAD AND ROLLS~YEAST

Superior, Quick Whole Wheat Bread

5½ cups lukewarm water
4 tbsp. yeast
½ cup oil
½ cup honey
½ cup gluten flour
2 tbsp. salt
¼ cup lecithin (liquid, powdered or granules)
¾ cup powdered whey
13-14 cups *unsifted* whole wheat flour

Measure lukewarm water into large 6-qt. container. Add yeast. Let stand until yeast begins to dissolve. Add oil, honey, gluten flour, salt, lecithin, whey and 6 cups flour. Beat thoroughly with spoon or electric mixer to make a "sponge." Let rest 10-15 minutes. Gradually stir in rest of flour. Knead well on floured breadboard. Let rest while greasing loaf pans (size above). Divide and form into 4 or 5 loaves, depending on pan size. Put in warm place to rise. If time permits, remold each loaf on board 1 or 2 additional times for extra fine texture. Cover with towel. Do not let dough rise in pans more than 3" to 3½" total height. Bake in preheated oven 350°-375° for 35-45 minutes. This recipe is excellent for a powerful electric mixer. (See Houseware Helps.)

Use same ingredients and beat 5 minutes to make the "sponge." Let rest 10-15 minutes. Add flour gradually until sides of bowl begin to come clean. Beat a few minutes longer. Oil hands and turn out on oiled kneading surface and proceed as above.

BREAD AND ROLLS~YEAST

Spoon Bread

1¾ cups warm milk
1 tbsp. yeast, dissolved in
⅓ cup lukewarm water
1 tbsp. oil
1-2 tbsp. honey or raw sugar
1½ tsp. salt
1 egg, beaten
3-3½ cups *unsifted* whole wheat flour

Add to warm milk the dissolved yeast, oil, sweetening, salt and egg. Add flour gradually. Beat vigorously after each addition and let rise at room temperature for 30 minutes. Stir down and spoon into greased loaf pan. Let rise 30 minutes or until not quite double in bulk. Bake 1 hour at 325°-350°.

Buttermilk Bread

1 tbsp. yeast, dissolved in
1 cup lukewarm water
3 tbsp. honey or brown sugar
2 tsp. salt
⅓ cup oil
1 cup buttermilk
¼ tsp. soda
3½-4 cups *unsifted* whole wheat flour

In a large bowl, dissolve yeast in lukewarm water. Let stand 5 minutes. Add honey, salt and oil. Stir soda into buttermilk and add to yeast mixture. Add flour, 1 cup at a time, beating well after each addition. Use no more flour than is necessary to make dough stiff enough to handle. Let rest 15 minutes. Knead well for 10 minutes. Cover and let rise in warm place until doubled in bulk. Mold into 1 large or 2 small loaves. Let rise until almost double in bulk. Bake 45-60 minutes at 350°, depending on size of loaf.

BREAD AND ROLLS – YEAST

Basic Whole Wheat Bread

Three 2-lb. or four 1½ lb. loaves.)

5 cups liquid*
2 tbsp. yeast, dissolved in
1 cup warm water
½ cup oil
½ cup raw sugar, honey or molasses
2 tbsp. salt
11-12 cups *unsifted* whole wheat flour

*Use water, potato water, fresh milk, diluted canned milk or noninstant powdered milk—1 cup powdered milk sifted with flour, then use plain water.

In 6-qt. container mix together, liquid, softened yeast, oil, sweetening and salt. Add flour gradually. Mix well, keeping it more moist than ordinary dough. Let rest 10-15 minutes. Knead 10 minutes (canvas-covered board, or greased hands and greased breadboard). Cover with lid, foil, or dampened towel. Refrigerate immediately 3-24 hours, depending on your time schedule. Rising bread may require "punching down." This "soak" prevents dry, crumbly bread. (Kneading can be done either before or after refrigeration.) Let cold dough stand 30-60 minutes at room temperature or in 80° to 85° oven.
(See Baking Hint No. 8.)

Divide into 3 2-lb. or 4 1½-lb. portions, depending on pan size. Mold loaves. Place in greased loaf pans. Let rise in warm place until almost double in bulk. Remold, if dough has risen more than double in bulk. Bake in preheated oven 400° for 30-40 minutes, or 350° for 50-60 minutes, or 325° for 1 hour. Turn out on rack to cool. Lightly butter tops for soft crust.

BREAD AND ROLLS~YEAST

Variations:

1. Raisin or date-nut bread may be made by adding to the dough of one of the loaves 1½ cups raisins or ½ lb. chopped dates and ½ to 1 cup nuts, plus 3 tbsp. raw sugar, if desired. Bake in 2 loaf pans or 2 cans (46-oz. juice cans).

2. For triple nutrition, add 1 tbsp. soy flour, 1 tbsp. noninstant powdered milk and 1 tsp. wheat germ to each cup of stoneground flour.

3. Old-fashioned sorghum is sometimes available and this used for sweetening gives the bread a different, delicious taste.

4. One cup cracked wheat or 1 cup bulgur may be added to Basic Bread recipe for a wholesome cracked wheat bread. If adding to Superior Quick Bread recipe, soak 1 cup bulgur in 1 cup water 2 hours.

5. Add a cooked cereal, such as cracked wheat or wheat germ (which has been cooked five minutes in milk) to the dough. This produces a more moist bread.

6. One cup whey powder may be substituted for the sweetening.

Electric Mixer Method: To streamline any bread or roll recipe, combine all ingredients except flour. Blend and add half the amount of flour and beat well until smooth and elastic for five minutes. (If your mixer will take more flour without overtaxing it or climbing the beaters, add more flour for the beating period.) Add balance of required flour gradually, kneading it in by hand. This beating cuts down the hand kneading time.

BREAD AND ROLLS~YEAST

Honey-Oatmeal Bread

1 cup rolled oats (old fashioned)
2 cups boiling water
2 tbsp. dry yeast, dissolved in
⅓ cup lukewarm water
6-6½ cups *sifted* whole wheat flour
½ cup powdered milk
2 tsp. salt
½ cup honey
¼ cup oil

Place rolled oats in large bowl. Add boiling water. Let stand until lukewarm (about 20 minutes). Sift together twice-powdered milk, salt and flour. Add dissolved yeast to oatmeal and let stand 5 minutes. Add honey and oil. then sifted dry ingredients. Knead well for five minutes. Let rise until double in bulk, then knead again. Shape into 2 loaves. Let rise 10 minutes in well-greased loaf pans. Bake 1 hour at 325°. Turn out and brush top with butter. This bread freezes well.

Variations:

Potato water may be used instead of plain water.

Add 1 cup raisins or 1 cup marmalade, and reduce honey to ¼ cup.

Add 1 cup cracked wheat, cooked or uncooked.

Add 1 cup cooked rice.

BREAD AND ROLLS~YEAST

No-Knead Raisin Bread

½ cup raw or brown sugar
⅓ cup soft margarine or butter
1 tsp. salt
½ cup boiling water
2 eggs, beaten
1 cup seedless raisins
1 cup canned milk
1 tbsp. yeast, dissolved in
¼ cup warm water
4-4½ cups *sifted* whole wheat flour
1 tbsp. raw or brown sugar
1 tsp. cinnamon

Mix sugar, butter and salt in large bowl. Add boiling water and stir until butter is melted. Add milk and dissolved yeast, eggs and raisins. Add flour, one cup at a time, beating until smooth after each addition. Cover and let rise until double in bulk. Then beat batter for 2 minutes. Turn into well-greased 10-inch tube pan, smoothing evenly with spoon. Let rise until almost double in bulk, about 45 minutes. Sprinkle top with sugar and cinnamon topping and bake 55 minutes at 350°.

Orange-Currant Loaf

1 tbsp. yeast, dissolved in
1½ cups warm water
⅓ cup oil
4 tsp. grated orange rind
½ cup raw or brown sugar
4-4½ cups *sifted* whole wheat flour
1½ tsp. salt
1 cup currants

Sift dry ingredients together. Add oil, orange rind, raw sugar to yeast mixture. Stir in dry ingredients. Add currants. Knead dough until smooth and elastic. Place in greased bowl Cover with damp cloth and let rise in warm place until double in bulk. Knead again for a few minutes, then mold into 2 loaves and place in greased loaf pans. Let rise again until almost double in bulk. Bake 50-60 minutes at 350°.

BREAD AND ROLLS~YEAST

Quick Two-Hour Buttercrust Bread

3 tbsp. yeast, dissolved in
3 cups warm water
⅓ cup honey
3 tbsp. oil
6-6½ cups *unsifted* whole wheat flour
1 tbsp. salt
1 cup powdered milk

Mix water, yeast, honey and oil in large bowl. Sift dry ingredients together and add to first mixture. Let stand in warm place for 15 minutes. Knead well for 10 minutes. Form into loaves and place in two well-greased loaf pans. Let rise 15 minutes in warm oven (80°-85°). Remove bread and heat oven to 350°-375°. Replace in oven and bake 50-55 minutes. Brush top with butter.

Easy Raisin Buns

1 tbsp. yeast, dissolved in
¾ cup warm water
⅓ cup raw or brown sugar
1 egg, beaten
¼ cup oil
1¾-2 cups *sifted* whole wheat flour
¾ tsp. salt
½ cup raisins

Combine beaten egg, dissolved yeast, sugar and oil. Add sifted flour and salt, then raisins and mix well. Knead and let rise in covered bowl until double in bulk. Knead down and form into buns. Place in greased 8" square pan. Let rise and bake 25-30 minutes at 375°. Frost if desired.

BREAD AND ROLLS~YEAST

Dilly Casserole Bread

1 tbsp. yeast, dissolved in
¼ cup warm water
1 cup cottage cheese, heated to lukewarm
2 tbsp. raw or brown sugar
2 tsp. instant minced onion
1 tbsp. butter or margarine
2 tsp. dill seeds
1 tsp. salt
1 beaten egg
2-2½ cups *sifted* whole wheat flour

Combine in mixing bowl cottage cheese, sugar, onion, butter, dill seed, salt, egg and softened yeast. Add flour gradually, beating well. Cover and let rise in warm place until light and double in bulk, 50-60 minutes. Stir down dough. Turn into well-greased 1-quart casserole and let rise in warm place until double in bulk. Bake 40-50 minutes at 350°, or until golden brown. Brush with softened butter and sprinkle with salt.

Delicious served warm with chili, etc.

Variations:

Omit cottage cheese and dill. Add a little milk if necessary.

BREAD AND ROLLS~YEAST

Herb Batter Bread

¾ cup canned milk
¾ cup boiling water
1 tsp. poppy seed
1 tsp. caraway seed
1 tsp. instant minced onion
1 tsp. dried chervil or parsley
½ tsp. marjoram or oregano
2 tbsp. raw or brown sugar
2 tsp. salt
4 tbsp. butter or margarine
2 tbsp. yeast, dissolved in
½ cup warm water
2 eggs, well-beaten
4-4½ cups *sifted* whole wheat flour

Combine water and canned milk. Add seeds, minced onion, herbs, sugar and salt. Stir in butter. Cool to lukewarm. Add dissolved yeast to first mixture. Add beaten eggs and flour. Beat vigorously for 2 minutes. Cover and let rise in warm place until more than double in bulk. Stir down with spoon, beating hard again for 1 minute. Turn into round, greased, 2-quart casserole. Let rise 5-10 minutes. Bake 40-45 minutes at 350°-375°. Brush with soft butter and sprinkle with salt.

Note: 1½ cups warm water may be substituted for canned milk and boiling water.

BREAD AND ROLLS~YEAST

Whole Wheat French Bread

This bread is delicious and very easy as it requires no kneading. All it takes is time. A laundry or ironing morning is ideal. Try it!

1 tbsp. yeast, dissolved in
2 cups warm water
2 tbsp. raw sugar or honey
1½ tsp. salt
2 tbsp. oil
4-4½ cups *sifted* whole wheat flour
Melted butter or margarine

In a large bowl, dissolve yeast in warm water. Add sweetening, salt and oil and stir well. Add sifted flour. Mix well with spoon. Cover bowl. Stir down dough at 10-minute intervals for five consecutive times. Turn dough onto lightly floured surface and divide in halves. Shape into 2 balls. Let rest 10 minutes, covered with towel.

Roll each ball into a 12" x 9" rectangle. Then roll firmly as for Jelly Roll, starting with the long side. Seal edge. Place rolls on well-greased baking sheet which has been sprinkled with cornmeal (optional). Make six diagonal slashes across top of each roll. Brush with cold water and let rise until almost double in bulk. Brush again with water. Sprinkle with sesame seed if desired. Bake 35-40 minutes at 375°-400°. Brush with melted butter while warm. Makes 2 loaves.

BREAD AND ROLLS~YEAST

It's All in the Way You Roll the Roll

PARKER HOUSE ROLLS: Roll dough ½" thick and cut with biscuit cutter. Dip in melted butter, fold, and press edges of round together. Place about ½" apart on pan or cookie sheet.

CLOVERLEAF ROLLS: (Form dough into balls about 1" in diameter. Place 3 balls in each greased muffin cup and brush with butter.

HAMBURGER ROLLS: Use a piece of dough about the size of an egg. Shape into ball and flatten slightly. These are delicious served with Spoon Burgers (in Meat Section).

HOT DOG ROLLS: Using a piece of dough about the size of an egg, roll between palms of hands into shape of a frankfurter and flatten slightly. Allow space for rising in pan.

BUTTERFLAKE ROLLS: Roll dough about ⅛" thick into 9" square. Spread with soft butter. Cut into 6 long strips 1½" wide. Stack 6 strips evenly on top of each other. Cut into 1" pieces. Place cut side down in greased muffin cups.

CRESCENTS: Using one-third of dough, roll out into an 8" circle. Cut into 12 wedge-shaped pieces like a pie. Starting at wide end, roll each wedge into a crescent or butterhorn shape. Place on well-greased cookie sheet, 2" apart. From the three portions, 36 rolls can be made. Bake on 2 cookie sheets to avoid crowding.

SWEET ROLLS: Roll out as for Jelly Roll and spread with mixture of ½ cup margarine, ½ cup brown sugar and grated rind of 3 oranges. Roll up and cut. Place in muffin tins.

MUFFINS: Bake in muffin cups, or roll muffin balls in mixture of ½ cup brown sugar and 1 tsp. cinnamon.

BREAD AND ROLLS~YEAST

Special Dinner Party Rolls

To be mixed day or morning before baking.)

2 tbsp. yeast, dissolved in
½ cup warm water
½ cup raw or brown sugar or honey
½ cup butter (no substitute)
½ cup boiling water
1 cup cold water
3 eggs, beaten
1½ tsp. salt
4-5 cups *sifted* whole wheat flour

Sift flour and salt together twice. Melt butter in ½ cup boiling water and add the 1 cup cold water. In large bowl combine sweetening and yeast mixture. Add dry ingredients, beating well. Cover with damp towel and let rise until double in bulk. Stir down. Replace dampened towel and place in *refrigerator*. Stir down several times as it continues to rise.

About 3 hours before serving time remove dough from refrigerator. Let stand at room temperature for ½ hour. Knead slightly on floured board and divide into 3 portions for convenient handling. Shape into type of rolls desired. Let rise about 2 hours or until double in bulk. Bake 12-15 minutes at 400°-425°. Makes about 3 dozen rolls.

BREAD AND ROLLS~YEAST

Refrigerator Rolls

2 tbsp. yeast, dissolved in
½ cup warm water
1 cup lukewarm milk (scald raw milk)
⅓ cup oil
⅓ cup raw or brown sugar
2 eggs, well-beaten
2 tsp. salt
4-4½ cups *unsifted* whole wheat flour

In large bowl combine milk, oil, sugar, eggs and salt. Add yeast mixture gradually. Add flour and mix well with spoon. Mixture will be sticky. Set in refrigerator several hours or overnight. Two hours before rolls are to be served, take dough from refrigerator and allow to stand at room temperature about 30 minutes. Knead well on board. Roll out and cut or shape as desired according to directions in "The Way You Roll the Roll." Place in pan and let rise about 1 hour. Bake 15-20 minutes at 375°-400°. This recipe will make about 32 Parker House rolls or 24 hamburger or hot dog rolls.

To make a delicious raisin or date-nut bread, double all ingredients except yeast and increase sugar to 1 cup. When ready to knead, add 3 cups raisins or 1 lb. dates and 1-2 cups chopped nuts. Shape into 3 loaves. Let rise for 1 hour at room temperature and bake 15-20 minutes at 325°-350°.

If large (46-oz.) juice cans are used to bake raisin or date-nut bread, the yield will be 4 round loaves. Bake 10-15 minutes longer than when using regular bread pans. Refer to Baking Hint No. 14.

BREAD AND ROLLS~YEAST

Quick Orange Glaze
(Can be used with any roll.)

1 tbsp. butter
2 tbsp. undiluted frozen orange concentrate
3 tbsp. raw or brown sugar

Combine in small saucepan and place over low heat, stirring until butter is melted and sugar is dissolved. Dip rolls into glaze. Bake according to specific roll recipe directions.

Basic Sweet Dough

2 tbsp. yeast, dissolved in
½ cup warm water
2 eggs, beaten
½ cup raw or brown sugar or honey
1 tsp. salt
½ cup oil, butter or margarine
1 tsp. grated lemon rind (optional)
½ cup canned milk
½ cup hot water
3½-4 cups *sifted* whole wheat flour

Combine beaten eggs, sweetening, salt, oil, lemon rind, canned milk and water. Stir in yeast mixture. Add flour, a small amount at a time, beating well. Add only sufficient flour to make a *soft* dough. Cover and let rest 10-15 minutes. Turn out on a lightly floured board, and knead well until surface is smooth and satiny and covered with tiny blisters. Place in greased bowl. Cover tightly and let rise until slightly more than double in bulk. Punch down and let rise 30 minutes. This second rising makes rolls with finer texture. Punch down and let rest 10 minutes. Shape into desired rolls or sweet bread. Cover and let rise in warm place (85°) until double in bulk. Bake 20-25 minutes at 350°-375°, for rolls. Bake loaves 25-35 minutes. Makes about 2½ dozen rolls.

BREAD AND ROLLS~YEAST

Cinnamon Rolls

Make Basic Sweet Dough. Roll dough into oblong sheet 9" x 18". Spread with 2 tbsp. softened butter and sprinkle with ½ cup raw or brown sugar, 2 tsp. cinnamon and ½ cup raisins. If desired, ½ cup chopped nuts can be added. Beginning with long side, roll dough as for a jelly roll, sealing edge by pinching with fingers. Better than a sharp knife, take string about 18" long. With an end in each hand, slip string under the roll to the cutting place. Bring string up and cross as if tying a knot. Pull string together and it will cut right through the roll without mashing or spoiling the shape. Place on greased cookie sheets, allowing for space for rising. Bake 25-30 minutes at 350°-375°. Frost if desired.

Cinnamon Roll Topping (instead of icing)

1 cup brown sugar
½ cup water

Bring to a full boil. Baste cinnamon rolls with this syrup before removing from pans to cool.

Swedish Tea Ring

Make Basic Sweet Dough. Prepare as for cinnamon rolls but do not slice. Place roll on greased baking sheet, joining ends of roll to form a ring. Seal ends well. With scissors, make cuts in roll about 1" apart. Cut each gash about ⅔ of the way across roll. Turn each section on side. Let rise and bake 25-30 minutes at 350°-375°. Frost, if desired.

Alternate Fruity Fillings: Use to fill tea rings, braids, and twists.

2 cups peeled, chopped apples
1 cup raisins
¼ tsp. salt
¼ cup water
½ tsp. cinnamon
½ cup brown sugar
½ cup chopped nuts (optional)

Boil together 3 minutes and cool until thick.

Filled Sweet Dough Ring

1 recipe Basic Sweet Dough
1 cup chopped dates
1 cup brown sugar
1 cup chopped nuts
1 tbsp. whole wheat flour
¼ cup water
½ cup orange juice
1 tsp. grated orange rind

Combine all ingredients for filling and cook over low heat about 10 minutes, or until thick. Cool. Proceed as for Swedish Tea Ring.

BREAD AND ROLLS~YEAST

Orange Rolls

Use Basic Sweet Dough. After second rising, roll dough into oblong sheet. Spread with filling made as follows:

1 cup raw or brown sugar
2 tsp. grated orange rind
½ cup orange juice
½ cup butter or margarine

Cook 2 minutes. Cool until thick and spread on roll dough. Roll as for cinnamon rolls. Cut and place on greased baking sheet. Let rise until double in bulk and bake about 25 minutes at 375°. Turn out on cake rack immediately.

Bohemian Bread

1 recipe Basic Sweet Dough
2 tsp. grated lemon rind
¼ tsp. mace
1 cup raisins
1 cup chopped nuts

After second rising of Basic Sweet Dough, knead in balance of ingredients. Divide dough into 3 equal parts and form each piece into a long roll. Place on baking sheet an inch apart and braid loosely, beginning at center and working toward ends. Seal ends well. Let rise until double in bulk. Bake 25-30 minutes at 350°-375°. Frost while still warm, if desired.

BREAD AND ROLLS~YEAST

Danish Coffee Twist

1 recipe Basic Sweet Dough
½ cup brown sugar
1½ tsp. cinnamon
2 tbsp. soft butter or margarine
Honey Glaze
½ cup slivered blanched almonds

Make Basic Sweet Dough. When dough has doubled, punch down. Shape into ball. Cover and let rest 5 minutes. While dough rests, mix sugar and cinnamon. Flatten ball of dough, then roll out to form long narrow sheet about 6" wide and ¼" thick. Spread with soft butter. Sprinkle with sugar-cinnamon mixture. Roll up to make long, slender roll. Seal edge by pressing firmly. Twist roll by pushing ends in opposite directions. Lift to lightly-buttered baking sheet and shape into large pretzel. Tuck ends of roll under edge of "pretzel" to keep dough from untwisting. Cover and let rise until doubled, about 1 hour. Bake 25-30 minutes at 350°. Brush hot glaze over twist as soon as it comes from oven. Sprinkle with slivered almonds. Remove from baking sheet to cooling rack. Makes one twist.

Honey Glaze

2 tbsp. raw or brown sugar
¼ cup honey
1 tbsp. butter or margarine

Place all ingredients in small saucepan and bring to boil, stirring constantly. While still hot, brush on baked Danish Coffee Twist.

BREAD AND ROLLS~YEAST

Russian Holiday Bread

1 recipe Basic Sweet Dough
1 cup raisins
¼ cup chopped almonds
1 tsp. grated lemon rind

Make Basic Sweet Dough. Stir in raisins, almonds and lemon rind before mixing in last cup of flour. Then finish mixing dough and knead. Shape into ball. Place in lightly buttered bowl. Cover and let rise until double in bulk. Punch down. Divide into 3 portions and shape into balls. Press each ball into well-buttered No. 2 can, into which a round of greased aluminum foil has been placed on the bottom. Cover and let rise until double in bulk. (It will rise a little above cans during baking). Bake 45-50 minutes at 350°. Turn out of cans immediately. When cool, frost top with powdered sugar frosting and decorate.

No-Knead Potato Refrigerator Rolls

1 tbsp. yeast, dissolved in
¼ cup lukewarm water
1 cup mashed potato
⅓ cup brown or raw sugar or honey
½ cup oil
2 tsp. salt
2 cups hot milk
2 eggs, beaten
5-5½ cups *sifted* whole wheat flour

Combine mashed potato, sweetening, oil, salt and hot milk. Cool to lukewarm. Stir in beaten eggs and dissolved yeast. Then add flour. Mix well, cover and let rise until double in bulk. Whip down, cover and place in refrigerator. Stir down as needed until chilled. About 1 hour before baking, spoon dough into 24 large muffin cups, filling them half full. Let rise until double in bulk. Bake 15-20 minutes at 375°.

Note: Potato flakes can be substituted. Use ½ cup potato flakes to 1 cup water.

BREAD AND ROLLS~YEAST

German Stollen

2 tbsp. yeast, dissolved in
½ cup warm water
2 eggs, beaten
½ cup canned milk
½ cup hot water
1 tsp. salt
½ cup honey or raw or brown sugar
½ cup oil, butter or margarine
1 tsp. grated lemon rind
3½-4 cups *sifted* whole wheat flour
½ cup chopped almonds
¼ cup candied citron, chopped
1½ tbsp. soft butter or margarine
3 tbsp. raw sugar
1 tsp. cinnamon

To beaten eggs, add milk, water, salt, sweetening, oil and lemon rind. Blend in yeast mixture. Add 3 cups of flour, a little at a time, beating well. Stir in almonds and candied fruit, then add rest of flour to make a soft dough. Cover and let rest 10-15 minutes. Knead well until surface is smooth and satiny. Place in greased bowl, cover, and let rise until slightly more than double in bulk. Punch down and let rise 30 minutes. Knead slightly and divide into two portions.

With hands, press dough into oval shape about ½" thick. Spread half of oval with soft butter, and sprinkle with mixture of sugar and cinnamon. Fold dough over the long way, forming into a crescent and press edges firmly together. Place on lightly greased baking sheet, curving ends slightly. Make second loaf the same way. Cover and let rise until double in bulk. Bake 35-40 minutes at 350°-375°. Remove from baking sheet. Cool, frost and decorate as desired.

BREAD AND ROLLS~YEAST

Russian Sweet Bread

3 tbsp. yeast, dissolved in
¾ cup warm water
4 eggs, beaten
1 tsp. salt
1 cup raw sugar or honey
¾ cup canned milk
4-4½ cups *sifted* whole wheat flour
¾ cup oil
1 cup chopped dates or raisins
2 tsp. grated lemon rind

Beat eggs in large mixing bowl. Add salt, sweetening, canned milk and dissolved yeast. Add 3 cups of whole wheat flour. Beat well with electric mixer. Add oil, about 2 tbsp. at a time, mixing well after each addition. Stir in remaining 1½ cups flour and beat batter by hand for about 5 minutes. Scrape batter from sides of bowl. Cover and let rise about 1½ hours until double in bulk. Stir down and add dates and grated lemon rind. Spoon carefully into well-greased tube pan, or two 1-qt. molds. Cover and let rise double in bulk. Bake 45 minutes at 350°. Turn out of pan and cool. Frost and garnish as desired.

BREAD AND ROLLS~YEAST

Braided Swiss Bread

2 tbsp. yeast, dissolved in
1 cup warm water
¾ cup canned milk
¾ cup water
½ cup honey
1 tbsp. salt
3 eggs, beaten
½ cup oil
6-6½ cups *sifted* whole wheat flour

In mixing bowl, combine dissolved yeast with milk, water, honey and salt. Add well-beaten eggs, oil and half of flour. Beat well and work in rest of flour with hands. Turn onto lightly floured board. Knead until smooth (about 5 minutes). Place in clean, buttered bowl; cover with damp cloth. Let rise until double in bulk. Punch down; let rise again 30 minutes.

Divide dough into thirds and then divide each third into thirds again to make nine strips. Roll each piece into long strips for braiding. Braid three strips loosely, working from center to ends. Pinch ends together securely. Repeat for rest of dough to make 3 loaves. Place on buttered baking sheet. Cover with damp cloth and let rise double in bulk, about 50-60 minutes. Bake 30-40 minutes at 350°. Frost if desired.

Variations:

One braided portion may be made 2" shorter. Then place on top of the larger braid.

Instead of frosting, use an Egg Yolk Glaze: With fork mix 1 egg yolk and 2 tbsp. cold water. Brush over bread just before baking. This makes a shiny, golden-brown finish.

BREAD AND ROLLS~YEAST

Yeast Corn Bread

1 tbsp. yeast, dissolved in
⅓ cup warm water
1½ cups *sifted* whole wheat flour
1½ cups yellow corn meal
⅓ cup noninstant powdered milk
1 tsp. salt
⅓ cup honey or raw or brown sugar
1 cup lukewarm milk
2 beaten eggs
⅓ cup oil or melted margarine

Sift together twice the flour, cornmeal, powdered milk and salt. Combine sweetening, milk, eggs, oil and dissolved yeast. Add dry ingredients to liquids and beat 25 strokes. Let rise in warm place 30 minutes. Stir down and pour into greased and floured 9" square pan. Let rise 10 minutes. Bake 30-35 minutes at 350°-375°.

Variations:

If bread is needed in a hurry, use up to three times as much yeast.

Bakes well in muffin cups. Fill half full and let rise. Bake 15-20 minutes.

If lighter texture is desired, use 2 eggs separated and fold in stiffly beaten egg whites just before baking.

BREAD AND ROLLS~YEAST

Yeast Raised Doughnuts

2 pkgs. yeast, dissolved in
½ cup lukewarm water
1 cup warm water
½ cup raw or brown sugar
¼ cup oil
3 well-beaten eggs
4-4½ cups *sifted* whole wheat flour
1 tsp. salt
⅓ cup noninstant powdered milk
¾ tsp. nutmeg

Combine in large bowl warm water, sugar, oil, eggs and dissolved yeast. Sift the dry ingredients together twice. Add to liquid mixture. Let stand 10 minutes. Turn out on lightly floured board or canvas and knead until smooth and elastic. Let rise until double in bulk. Roll out ½" thick and cut with floured doughnut cutter. Arrange the rings well apart on lightly floured cookie sheets. Cover with tea towel and let rise in warm place until almost double in bulk.

Meanwhile, heat oil in deep fryer or saucepan to 375°. Fry the raised doughnuts a few at a time, turning them once until golden brown. Do not prick doughnuts with a fork. Drain on absorbent paper. These are best served warm or reheated.

BREAD AND ROLLS~YEAST

Sesame Buns

2 tbsp. yeast
2½ cups warm water
2 tbsp. honey
2 tsp. salt
6-6½ cups *sifted* whole wheat flour
1 slightly beaten egg white
1 tbsp. water
sesame seeds

Soften yeast in warm water. Add honey. Add 3 cups sifted flour and salt. Beat well. Let stand 10 minutes. Add remainder of flour. Dough will be stiffer than ordinary bread dough. Knead well 10-15 minutes or until very elastic. Place dough in lightly greased bowl, turning once to greased surface. Cover and let rise in warm place until double in bulk. Punch down. Let rise again until double in bulk. Punch down. Turn out on canvas board. Cover with warm, damp cloth and let rest 10 minutes.

Divide into 24 portions. Shape each into oval or round rolls. Place 2" apart on greased cookie sheets. Add 1 tbsp. water to slightly beaten egg white. Brush over tops and sides of rolls, covering well with fingers or brush. Sprinkle generously with sesame seeds. Let rise in warm place until double in size. Bake 20 minutes at 375°.

Note: To make them still better, substitute ½ cup gluten flour for ½ cup whole wheat flour. After punching down second time, turn out on canvas board and form 24 rolls. Let rise until double in size and brush with egg white and sesame seeds and bake as above.

BREAD AND ROLLS~YEAST

Yeast Waffles

(Waffles and pancakes are more nutritious when made with yeast rather than baking powder and can be made almost as quickly.)

1 tbsp. yeast, dissolved in
½ cup water
2 tbsp. honey
1½ cups sweet or sour milk, buttermilk, or yogurt
3 eggs, separated
⅔ cup oil
½ cup fresh wheat germ (optional)
1½ cups *sifted* whole wheat flour
½ cup noninstant powdered milk
½ tsp. salt

Combine water, sweetening and yeast in mixing bowl. Let stand 5 minutes. Stirring well, add milk, egg yolks, oil and wheat germ. Sift in flour, powdered milk and salt and blend. Let rise in warm place for 2 hours or longer, stirring down each time batter has doubled in bulk. Just before baking, fold in stiffly beaten egg whites. Bake on preheated waffle iron. Serve with applesauce, fresh raspberries or strawberries.

Note: If more convenient, mix batter at night. Let rise once or twice. Stir down and set in refrigerator overnight. Remove from refrigerator 30 minutes before baking.

Pancakes

By adding ½ cup more liquid to above Waffle recipe, you produce a batter which makes delicious pancakes.

BREAD AND ROLLS~QUICK

Orange Bread

Peelings from 3 or 4 medium-size oranges
1 cup raw or brown sugar
¾ cup water

Boil together orange peelings, sugar and water 15 minutes. Cool and grind. This should make 2 cups pulp.

4 cups *sifted* whole wheat flour
3 tsp. baking powder
1 tsp. salt
½ cup raw or brown sugar
½ cup butter or margarine
2 eggs, beaten
1⅓ cups milk
1 cup nuts (optional)

Sift together, twice, the flour, baking powder and salt. Cream sugar, eggs, shortening. Add milk with dry ingredients. Add pulp and beat all together. Bake in 2 greased loaf pans 70-80 minutes at 325°-350°.

Apple Loaf

2 cups *sifted* whole wheat flour
1½ tsp. baking powder
½ tsp. salt
½ cup margarine
⅔ cup raw or brown sugar
2 eggs
1 cup ground raw apple (unpeeled)
¼ cup chopped nuts

Sift together, twice, the flour, baking powder and salt. Cream butter and sugar. Add eggs and beat well. Add sifted dry ingredients, apples and nuts. Blend well. Pour into greased loaf pan and bake 60-70 minutes at 325°-350°.

BREAD AND ROLLS~QUICK

Applesauce-Banana Bread

2 cups *sifted* whole wheat flour
½ tsp. soda
1 tsp. baking powder
½ tsp. salt
½ cup butter or margarine
¾ cup raw or brown sugar
2 eggs, well beaten
3 tbsp. buttermilk or sour milk
1 medium-size banana, mashed, plus enough applesauce to make 1 cup

Sift together dry ingredients twice. Cream together butter and sugar. Add eggs, sour milk and banana-applesauce mixture. Add dry ingredients. Blend well and pour into greased loaf pan. Bake 1 hour at 350°-375°.

Canadian Banana Bread

1 cup brown sugar
½ cup margarine or butter
1 tsp. vanilla
3 large ripe bananas, mashed
2 eggs, well beaten
2 cups *sifted* whole wheat flour
3 tsp. baking powder
½ tsp. salt
½ cup chopped nuts

Cream sugar and margarine. Add vanilla and mashed bananas, then eggs. Sift dry ingredients together twice and add to creamed mixture. Add nuts. Pour into one large or two small loaf pans and bake 1 hour at 325°-350°.

BREAD AND ROLLS~QUICK

Orange Marmalade Quick Bread

1 cup orange marmalade
3 tsp. baking powder
¾ tsp. salt
3 cups sifted whole wheat flour
2 eggs, slightly beaten
1 cup milk
3 tbsp. oil
1 cup nuts (optional)

Heat marmalade in saucepan until liquefied. Cool. Sift together dry ingredients twice. Combine beaten eggs, milk and oil. Add marmalade then dry ingredients. Blend well Bake in well-greased and floured loaf pan 1 hour at 350°. Let "ripen" for 1 day before slicing.

Nut Bread

3 cups sifted whole wheat flour
4 tsp. baking powder
¾ tsp. salt
1 cup milk
¾ cup raw or brown sugar
1 egg, beaten
1 tsp. vanilla
1 cup chopped nuts

Sift flour, baking powder and salt together twice into mixing bowl. Add milk, sugar, egg, vanilla and nuts. Pour into greased loaf pan and bake 60-70 minutes at 325°-350°.

Note: One cup raisins may be added to make Raisin-Nut Bread.

BREAD AND ROLLS~QUICK

Prune Bread

2 cups *sifted* whole wheat flour
2½ tsp. baking powder
½ tsp. soda
½ tsp. salt
½ cup raw or brown sugar
½ cup oil
1 egg, beaten
1 cup quick-cooking oatmeal
1 cup buttermilk
¾ cup pitted, cooked prunes, drained and coarsely cut
½ cup walnuts

Sift together, twice, the flour, baking powder, soda and salt. Cream together sugar and oil. Add egg and oatmeal. Add sifted dry ingredients alternately with buttermilk. Add prunes and nuts. Pour into greased loaf pan and bake 70-80 minutes at 325°-350°.

Date-Nut Bread

2 cups boiling water
1 tsp. soda
2 cups chopped dates
2 tbsp. butter or margarine
4 cups *sifted* whole wheat flour
½ tsp. salt
2 tsp. cinnamon
3 tsp. baking powder
2 eggs, beaten
2 cups raw or brown sugar
2 tsp. vanilla
1 cup chopped nuts

In mixing bowl combine boiling water and soda, then add dates and butter. Sift together, twice, the flour, cinnamon, baking powder and salt. Add beaten eggs and sugar. Add dry ingredients, then vanilla and nuts. Grease 2 loaf pans and line bottoms with waxed paper. Pour into pans and let stand 5 minutes before baking about 75 minutes at 325°-350°. This bread is better if baked the day before it is used.

BREAD AND ROLLS~QUICK

Oatmeal Spice Bread

2 cups *sifted* whole wheat flour
4 tsp. baking powder
¾ tsp. salt
¼ tsp. ginger
¼ tsp. nutmeg
¼ tsp. cinnamon
½ cup raw or brown sugar
1 cup quick-cooking oatmeal
1 cup milk
2 eggs, well beaten
1 tsp. vanilla
⅓ cup oil
½ cup honey or molasses

Into mixing bowl sift together, twice, the flour, baking powder, salt and spices. Stir in brown sugar and oatmeal. Make a well in dry ingredients. Combine remaining ingredients and pour into well, stirring just enough to blend. Do not overmix.

Grease a large loaf pan. Line bottom with waxed paper and grease the paper. Bake 45-50 minutes at 350°. Turn out and cool. Store for 24 hours, wrapped in foil. Slice and serve with butter or creamed cheese.

Deluxe Hot Cakes

1½ cups *sifted* whole wheat flour
1 tbsp. baking powder
¾ tsp. salt
3 tbsp. raw or brown sugar
2 eggs, separated
1½ cups whole milk
3 tbsp. oil

Sift together, twice, the flour, baking powder, salt and sugar. Beat egg yolks, milk and oil. Combine with sifted dry ingredients. Fold in beaten egg whites last. Bake on lightly greased, hot griddle.

BREAD AND ROLLS~QUICK

Spiced Applesauce-Currant Loaf

4 cups *sifted* whole wheat flour
4 tsp. baking powder
1 tsp. salt
2 tsp. cinnamon
½ tsp. nutmeg
¼ tsp. cloves
2 cups raw or brown sugar
1 cup margarine or butter
1 tsp. vanilla
1 tsp. lemon extract
4 eggs, well beaten
2 cups applesauce
1 cup currants
1 cup chopped nuts

Sift together, twice, the flour, baking powder, salt and spices. Cream sugar and butter together and add flavorings, eggs and applesauce. Add dry ingredients. Blend until smooth. Stir in nuts and currants. Turn into 2 large loaf pans or 4 small ones. Bake 1 hour at 350°, or until bread tests done. Cool at least 4 hours before slicing.

Dried Apricot Bread

1 cup dried apricots
2 cups *sifted* whole wheat flour
3 tsp. baking powder
¼ tsp. salt
1 cup raw or brown sugar
4 tbsp. soft butter or margarine
2 eggs, beaten
¼ cup water
½ cup orange juice
½ cup chopped nuts

Soak apricots in warm water to cover for 30 minutes. Drain and cut in pieces with scissors. Sift together, twice, the flour, baking powder and salt. Cream sugar and butter. Add beaten egg. Add dry ingredients alternately with orange juice and water. Add chopped nuts and apricots. Bake in greased loaf pan, lined on bottom with waxed paper, 50-55 minutes at 350°.

BREAD AND ROLLS~QUICK

Date-Nut Orange Bread

3 cups *sifted* whole wheat flour
½ tsp. salt
3 tsp. baking powder
½ cup margarine or butter
¾ cup raw or brown sugar
1 tsp. vanilla
2 eggs, beaten
1 tbsp. grated orange peel
¾ cup sour milk or buttermilk
½ cup orange juice
1 cup chopped dates
1 cup chopped nuts

Sift together, twice, the flour, salt and baking powder. Cream butter and sugar. Add vanilla, eggs and orange peel. Beat until light and fluffy. Add dry ingredients alternately with sour milk and orange juice. Beat well after each addition. Fold in chopped dates and nuts. Pour into 1 large or 2 small, well-greased loaf pans. Bake 50-60 minutes at 350°. Cool thoroughly before slicing.

Corn Bread

1 cup *sifted* whole wheat flour
4 tsp. baking powder
¾ tsp. salt
1 cup yellow cornmeal
¼ cup raw or brown sugar
2 eggs, beaten
1 cup milk
¼ cup oil

Sift together, twice, the flour, baking powder and salt into mixing bowl. Stir in cornmeal and sugar. Add eggs, milk and oil. Beat until barely smooth, about 1 minute. Do not overbeat. Pour into greased 9" square pan. Bake 25 minutes at 425°. Serve hot with butter.

BREAD AND ROLLS~QUICK

Boston Brown Bread

2 cups *sifted* whole wheat flour
1 cup yellow cornmeal
1 tsp. salt
3 tsp. baking powder
¾ cup molasses
2 cups buttermilk or sour milk
1 cup seedless raisins

Sift dry ingredients together into mixing bowl. Add molasses, buttermilk and raisins. Beat well. Divide batter into four 1-lb. cans, well-greased and floured. Cover cans tightly with double layer of foil. Place on rack or folded towel in deep kettle. Pour in water to 2" depth and cover kettle. Steam three hours, adding more water, if necessary. Uncover cans and place in very hot oven, 450° for 5 minutes. Remove bread from cans and cool.

Muffins

2 cups *sifted* whole wheat flour
½ tsp. salt
3 tsp. baking powder
2 eggs
1 cup milk
3 tbsp. raw or brown sugar
2 tbsp melted butter or oil

Sift together, twice, the flour, salt and baking powder. Combine beaten eggs, milk, sugar and oil. Stir in dry ingredients only until flour mixture is absorbed. Bake in greased muffin tins 20-30 minutes at 375°-400°.
For a richer muffin, increase sugar to ⅓ cup and oil to ¼ cup.

Variations:

Blueberry muffins: Add ¾ cup fresh or frozen blueberries, or well-drained canned berries.

Date or nut muffins: Add ½ cup dates or nuts.

Old-fashioned cornmeal muffins: Substitute 1 cup cornmeal for 1 cup whole wheat flour.

BREAD AND ROLLS~QUICK

Steamed Honey-Date or Honey-Raisin Bread

2 cups cracked wheat
3 cups buttermilk or sour milk
1 cup honey
1 cup rye flour
2 cups *sifted* whole wheat flour
1 cup yellow cornmeal
4 tsp. baking powder
1½ tsp. salt
1 tsp. allspice
1 lb. dates or raisins

In mixing bowl soak cracked wheat in buttermilk and honey 30 minutes. Sift dry ingredients together and add to cracked wheat mixture. Stir in dates or raisins. Grease two 46-oz. juice cans, place a round of foil in bottom of can and grease well. Spoon in batter and cover tightly with double layers of foil large enough to extend halfway down sides of cans. Place cans on rack or folded towel in deep kettle, and add boiling water to 3" depth. Cover with tight lid and steam 3 hours, adding more water if necessary. Uncover cans and place in 450° oven 5 minutes. Remove bread from cans and cool. Freezes well and is delicious toasted.

Note: If rye flour is not available, use a total of 3 cups whole wheat flour.

Baking Powder Biscuits

2 cups *sifted* whole wheat flour
¾ tsp. salt
4 tsp. baking powder
6 tbsp. butter or margarine
⅔ cup milk (about)

Sift together flour, salt and baking powder. Cut in butter with pastry blender. Mix in just enough milk to make soft dough—not too wet. Turn out on lightly floured board. Pat out to ½"-¾" thickness. Cut with floured cutter. Bake on greased cookie sheet 15-20 minutes at 375°-400°. Makes 12-16 biscuits.

BREAD AND ROLLS ~ QUICK

Six-Week Bran Muffins

2 cups 40 percent Bran cereal
4 cups All-Bran cereal
2 cups boiling water
1 quart buttermilk
1 cup butter or margarine
2½ cups raw or brown sugar
4 eggs, beaten
1 cup chopped nuts
5 cups *sifted* whole wheat flour
5 tsp. soda
½ tsp. salt

Combine cereals and boiling water. Let stand a few minutes. Add buttermilk. Cream and sugar. Add beaten eggs and nuts. Sift together flour, soda and salt. Combine all ingredients and stir just until blended. Will store in refrigerator for 6 weeks. Bake amount needed in greased muffin cups 15-20 minutes at 400°.

All-Bran Muffins

1 cup All-Bran
¾ cup milk
1 cup *sifted* whole wheat flour
¼ tsp. salt
2 tsp. baking powder
½ cup raw or brown sugar or honey
2 tbsp. oil
1 egg
½ cup raisins (optional)

Combine All-Bran and milk. Sift together, twice, the flour, salt and baking powder. Mix sweetening, oil and egg and beat hard for 1 minute. Add sifted dry ingredients and All-Bran mixture and beat until smooth. Add raisins. Spoon into 12 muffin tins and bake 15-20 minutes at 400°.

BREAD AND ROLLS~QUICK

Baking Powder Cinnamon Rolls

2 cups *sifted* whole wheat flour
¼ tsp. salt
4 tsp. baking powder
2 tbsp. raw or brown sugar
½ cup shortening
2 eggs
½ cup milk
2 tbsp. melted butter
½ cup raw or brown sugar
1 tsp. cinnamon
1 tbsp. milk

Sift together, twice, the flour, salt, baking powder and sugar into mixing bowl. With pastry blender cut in shortening to resemble coarse crumbs. Beat one whole egg and egg white, reserving 1 yolk for topping. Combine beaten egg and milk and add to dry ingredients. Blend well with fork. Turn out on lightly greased surface and knead ½ minute. Roll out in rectangular shape ¼" thick. Brush with melted butter. Sprinkle with sugar and cinnamon mixed. Roll as for jelly roll and cut in ½" slices. Place in shallow greased pan. Brush with mixture of beaten egg yolk and 1 tbsp. milk. Sprinkle sparsely with sugar and cinnamon. Bake 15-20 minutes at 375°-400°.

French Toast

3 eggs
⅔ cup milk
¼ tsp. salt
6 slices whole wheat bread

Beat eggs. Add milk and salt. Dip each slice of bread in liquid mixture and fry in hot oil.

BREAD AND ROLLS~QUICK

Irish Soda Scone

4 cups sifted whole wheat flour
4 tsp. baking powder
1½ tsp. salt
¼ cup brown sugar
½ cup rolled oats
⅓ cup margarine
1 tsp. baking soda
3 tbsp. hot water
1¾ cups buttermilk
1 cup chopped dates or raisins (optional)

Grease a 10" frying pan (suitable for oven) or cookie sheet. Preheat oven to 400°. Sift flour, baking powder and salt together into a mixing bowl. Mix in brown sugar and rolled oats. Cut in margarine with pastry blender until it resembles coarse meal. Mix in dates or raisins. Dissolve baking soda in hot water. Add to buttermilk and stir well. Make a well in dry ingredients. Add liquid and combine with fork, adding a little more buttermilk if necessary to make a stiff dough. Knead 10 times.

If scone is being baked in greased frying pan, just pat out evenly with hands. If baking on a cookie sheet, pat or roll into 10" circle. Score almost through dough, with floured knife to mark 4 quarters. Bake 30-35 minutes at 400°. While still hot, brush with milk and a little raw or brown sugar, if desired.

Waffles (extremely light)

1 cup *sifted* whole wheat flour
3 tsp. baking powder
½ tsp. salt
2 tsp. raw or brown sugar
2 eggs, separated
1¼ cups milk
¼ cup oil

Sift together, 3 times, the flour, baking powder, salt and sugar. Add egg yolks, oil and milk gradually. Batter will be very thin. Beat hard for 2 minutes. Fold in beaten egg whites. Bake in preheated waffle iron. Serve with applesauce and table cream or your favorite topping.

BREAD AND ROLLS~QUICK

Breakfast Sweet Bread

2 cups Wheatquick Mix No. 1
¼ cup raw or brown sugar
2 eggs, slightly beaten
¾ cup water or milk
½ cup raisins
½ cup brown sugar
½ cup chopped nuts

Blend Wheatquick Mix and sugar together. Combine eggs and milk and stir into mix. Add raisins. Pour into greased 9" square pan. Combine brown sugar and cinnamon and sprinkle on top, adding nuts if desired. Bake 35-40 minutes at 350°. Serve hot.

Wheatquick Mix No. 1

8 cups *unsifted* whole wheat flour
¼ cup baking powder, plus 2 tsp.
4 tsp. salt
2 cups shortening
⅓ cup raw or brown sugar

Sift dry ingredients together twice. Cut in shortening with pastry blender. Store in covered jar in refrigerator and mix as needed. It will keep for 1-2 months. When using for biscuits use about ¼-½ cup milk to 1 cup of Wheatquick. For biscuits bake 12-15 minutes at 375°-400°. Use as you would a commercial biscuit mix—a real convenience.

Note: To make delicious hot cakes, beat one egg, add 1 tbsp. raw sugar and 1 cup milk. Beat in 1¼ cups Wheatquick and bake on hot griddle. This is ideal for camping trips.

Two cups powdered milk may be added to the basic ingredients above, then use water instead of milk for mixing.

BREAD AND ROLLS~QUICK

Wheatquick Mix No. 2

6 cups *sifted* whole wheat flour
2 cups soy flour
1¾ tbsp. salt
⅓ cup double-acting baking powder
1 cup noninstant powdered milk
½ to 1 cup wheat germ

Sift together into large bowl the flour, salt, baking powder and powdered milk. Add the wheat germ and mix thoroughly. Store in refrigerator or freezer until needed. Use this mix by merely substituting it for the amount of flour called for in your favorite recipes and omit the salt and baking powder or soda. Spices may be blended into the dry mix before liquids are added. Even if the recipe you use calls for sour milk or buttermilk, it isn't necessary to use soda, as the protein in the mix will neutralize the acid.

Note: Since flours vary considerably in moisture content, you may find the batter too thin and will need to add more mix; or it may be too thick and you will need more liquid. There is no limit to the use of these two mixes; i.e., pancakes, waffles, biscuits, muffins.

MEATS~CASSEROLES

Gluten

For your convenience, some of the information given earlier for making gluten flour will be repeated here together with what you need to know to use gluten in protein dishes.

Gluten can be made by hand or in an electric dough mixer. When making by hand, use the basic amounts given below and knead thoroughly a good 10 minutes, pounding and rolling dough also to develop the gluten completely. Then follow all the other instructions outlined below after the words *"take out dough hook."*

Electric dough mixer method:

   9 cups cold water in mixer bowl
   18 cups fine whole wheat stoneground flour

To the water in mixer bowl, add 6 cups flour, beating until well blended. Then add another 6 cups. The last six cups must be sprinkled in slowly because of stiffness. Moisture content will vary with different wheat. Be careful that dough doesn't clean the bowl as in breadmaking. If it gets to that point, add a little water to restore moisture. Knead 5-10 minutes. Remove bowl from its base and *take out dough hook.*

Add 2" of water on top of dough. With hands clean it away from sides and bottom of bowl. Pour first starch water off into another pan. Save all water from gluten-making because it contains vitamins and minerals. Use it for breadmaking, mixing dry milk, gravies, soups, sauces, eggnog, banana drink, frozen fruit ices, etc.

Set colander containing many small holes in pan of water. Add about 2 cups of dough at a time to colander. In pan squeeze fingers into dough and pull it away from holes. It will seem to come apart and you think you'll lose it. Then suddenly it will act like bubble gum. Pick it up with both hands and, in a second pan, squeeze it under the cleaner water until the sandy feeling is gone. (Water should

MEATS~CASSEROLES

run clear.) Set it aside and let rest in another colander at least a half hour to drain off as much moisture as possible.

Raw gluten can be prepared as a substitute for meat in a variety of ways:* and can be prepared and refrigerated or frozen for future use.

1. *Ground "beef,"* to be used for patties, meatballs, casseroles, etc. Place raw gluten on lightly oiled cookie sheet or 2-3 bread pans. Push from the center out and stretch until it is fairly even, ½" thick. Bake 15 minutes in preheated oven at 350°. Twist fork in bubbles and thick-raised areas to let out steam. Cook another 15 minutes or until it springs back when pressed.

Remove from oven and if gluten seems crisp on top or bottom, either put it in a plastic bag or fold the large sheet of gluten until the steam adjusts the texture evenly, or sprinkle water on it. When there are no crisp areas, run it through the meat grinder on medium disk, or grate on largest holes of a shredder. It will be soft and pliable. Refrigerate or freeze for future use in hamburger, sauces, patties, sausages, casseroles or desserts.

To make hamburger, place ground gluten in a bowl. Season with dried onion soup powder. Stir in egg and chopped or dried onion. (Dried onion soup mix may be used.) Brown in oil in a skillet. Cover and slowly steam 5 minutes to bring out flavor.

2. *Cutlets and steaks*: Bake raw gluten in a greased No. 2 size can. After it has rested, push it down so that air bubbles disappear. Bake uncovered at 250° 90 minutes, or until it springs back to the touch. Cool. Remove from can and slice ¼" thick—10 slices per 2 cups raw gluten.

*See *The Gluten Book,* by LeArta Moulton, published by The Gluten Co., Inc., Box 482 Provo, Utah 84601.

MEATS~CASSEROLES

Put gluten slices in boiling broth made with 2 cups water, 2 tbsp. bouillon powder (or 2 cubes), 2 tsp. soy sauce, 1 tsp. Worcestershire sauce and 1 tsp. Kitchen Bouquet. Liquid should just barely cover gluten. Simmer 60-90 minutes, until broth is almost gone and pieces are firm rather than rubbery. Press out as much liquid as possible with spoon or strainer, or blot with paper towel. Place steaks or cutlets on cookie sheet and bake 30 minutes at 300° to dry out. After 15 minutes of cooking, turn them over.

Dip pieces in beaten egg, milk or oil and "bread" in bread crumbs or flour. Fry with oil in skillet until browned on both sides.

3. *Roast.* Put ball of raw gluten in beef-flavored liquid (as in No. 2 Steaks) enough to cover well. Cover pan with lid and let simmer 8 hours, being sure it does not go dry. Alternatively it can be baked 8 hours at 250°. Slice thin and serve hot as roast beef.

4. *Stew cubes.* Roll out raw gluten ½" thick with rolling pin. Cut into cubes with scissors. Drop gluten pieces into boiling sauce made, as follows:

In 4-quart kettle lightly brown 1 large chopped onion in ½ cup oil. Add 1 tbsp. seasoned salt or Vege-Sal. Drop in gluten cubes and add 1½ quarts boiling water and 2 bay leaves. Boil gently 1 hour. Lift out of pan carefully with slotted spoon and drain. Save liquid for soups or stews. At this point cubes will be spongy. Press out liquid and bake 30 minutes at 300° until firm and chewy.

Add to simmering stew, gravy, casserole about 20 minutes before serving. When used in Glorified Stew, or in any other casserole recipe calling for stew meat, follow recipe, using about 2 cups stew cubes for each pound of stew meat required in recipe.

MEATS~CASSEROLES

Seasoned Flour

Delicious and convenient to have for dredging any meat requiring dusting or flouring.

2 cups whole wheat flour
2 tbsp. salt
1 tbsp. celery salt
1 tbsp. pepper
2 tbsp. dry mustard
4 tbsp. paprika
½ tsp. ginger
½ tsp. thyme
½ tsp. sweet basil
½ tsp. oregano or marjoram

In large bowl, combine all seasonings with 1 cup flour. Mix well. Blend in last cup of flour. When dredging meat for stew, Swiss steak, cutlets, fish, etc., use equal amounts of seasoned flour and whole wheat flour.

Note: For delicious chicken, beat together 1 egg and ½ cup milk; dip chicken in liquid, then dredge with seasoned flour.

Casserole Steak

Pound whole wheat flour into round steak. Brown in fat. Salt. Almost cover with water. Add large sliced onion. Cook *very* slowly for 2 hours.

Cubed Steak

1 lb. cubed steak
1 tsp. salt
¼ cup whole wheat flour
6 tbsp. oil
1½ cups hot water
1 medium size onion

Mix flour and salt and use all of it to dredge steak. Brown meat in oil in frying pan. Remove to casserole. Add water to frying pan. Bring to boil, making a gravy. Season to taste. Pour over meat. Add sliced onion. Bake 1 hour at 350°.

MEATS ~ CASSEROLES

Beef Short Ribs

2 lb. beef short ribs
½ cup whole wheat flour (about)
2 tbsp. oil
2 tsp. salt
⅛ tsp. pepper
½ cup water
½ onion
½ green pepper, if desired
2 carrots, cut in 1" pieces
2 stalks celery, cut in 1" pieces

Cut short ribs into individual servings and flour them. Brown slowly in hot oil (20-30 minutes). Add seasonings, water and finely cut onion. Cover and simmer 1¼ hours. Add vegetables and continue to cook 1 hour. Remove meat to platter. Thicken vegetable gravy with 1 tbsp. whole wheat flour stirred into ½ cup water.

Stuffed Lamb or Pork Chops

6 loin or rib lamb chops, 1½" thick or 6 pork chops, 1½" thick
¼ cup oil
¼ cup chopped celery
2 tbsp. finely chopped onion
2 cups soft whole wheat bread crumbs
½ tsp. salt
⅛ tsp. pepper
1 tbsp. lemon juice (for lamb)
½ grated apple (for pork)

With sharp knife, split chops through middle from outer edge to bone. Spread open. Sauté celery and onion in oil until lightly browned. Blend in remaining ingredients. Fill split in chop with 1-2 tbsp. dressing. Roast chops, uncovered, in shallow baking dish at 350° for 30 minutes. Season with salt and pepper. Repeat on other side. Roast until tender.

MEATS~CASSEROLES

Roasted Meat

Any cut of meat suitable for roasting or pot roast may be rubbed with salt and pepper and dredged with whole wheat flour. Sprinkle with 1 tbsp. Worcestershire sauce if desired. May use bay leaf and onion slices. Roast or pot roast in usual manner.

Swiss Steak

2 lb. round steak, cut 1" thick
½ cup whole wheat flour
1½ tsp. salt
¼ tsp. pepper
2 cups sliced onions
3 tbsp. oil
1½ cups canned tomatoes

This cooks well in electric frying pan. Wipe off meat; trim off excess fat. Combine flour, salt and pepper. Pound into both sides of steak with a meat mallet or edge of heavy plate. Cook onions in oil until tender; remove from pan. Brown steak on both sides, adding more oil if necessary. Cover with onions and add tomatoes. Cover pan tightly and cook just below boiling point until tender (2-2½ hours).

Variation:

Tomatoes may be omitted and meat removed from frying pan while a gravy is being made with 2 cups warm water. Bring to good boil. If more thickening is needed add in form of whole wheat flour and water stirred into a paste. Season to taste. Add meat and cook according to directions above.

MEATS ~ CASSEROLES

Spoon-Burgers (Sloppy-Joes)

3 lb. ground beef
2 large onions, chopped
1 tbsp. flour
1 tsp. salt
1 tbsp. chili powder
3 tbsp. ketchup
4 tsp. Worcestershire sauce
2 cans tomato soup
3 bay leaves

Brown meat and chopped onion in deep skillet. Add all other ingredients and simmer 30-45 minutes. Remove bay leaves. Spoon onto hamburger buns made from Superior Quick Bread recipe. Serves approximately 25.

Hamburgers

1 lb. ground meat
1 large onion, chopped fine
1 tsp. salt
3 tbsp. whole wheat flour

Combine all ingredients and add enough water or tomato juice to hold ingredients together, starting with $1/4$ cup. Mix well. Form into patties, brown and cook.

Hamburger Gravy

1 lb. hamburger
2 medium size onions
$1/2$ cup whole wheat flour
4 cups water
1 tsp. salt
dash pepper
1 tsp. Worcestershire sauce or $1/2$ tsp. Kitchen Bouquet

Brown hamburger and chopped onions, using additional fat if necessary. Turn often so that meat is broken up well (as for chili). Stir in $1/2$ cup whole wheat flour. Add water and seasonings and cook slowly for 20 minutes. Serve over potatoes or toasted whole wheat bread.

MEATS~CASSEROLES

Hamburger Meatballs

2 slices stale whole wheat bread
¾ cup milk
1 lb. hamburger
1 egg, beaten
1 onion, chopped fine
1 tsp. salt
¼ tsp. pepper
½ cup whole wheat flour
2 tbsp. oil
½ cup water
2½ cups tomatoes
2 medium size onions, sliced

Soak bread in milk 1 hour, until very soft. Mix meat, softened bread, beaten egg, finely-chopped onion, salt and pepper. Form into small meat balls. Roll in flour and brown in hot oil. Put in large casserole. Pour ½ cup water in frying pan and stir to dissolve juices; then pour over meat balls. Add tomatoes and onions finely sliced. Season with salt if needed. Cover and simmer at 350° for 1 hour; reduce heat to 325° and continue to simmer 1 hour more.

Danish Frikadeller (Beef Patties)

1 lb. ground beef
½ lb. pork sausage
½ medium onion, finely chopped
2 eggs, beaten
1 cup canned milk
1 cup whole wheat flour
1 tsp. salt
¼ tsp. pepper
¼ tsp. nutmeg
½ tsp. mace

Combine ingredients and drop by heaping tablespoons into hot, generously oiled frying pan. Pat with spoon to ¾" thick. Fry as you would hamburgers.

MEATS~CASSEROLES

Hamburgers with Barbecue Sauce

1½ lb. ground beef
½ tsp. salt
⅛ tsp. pepper
¾ cup dry whole wheat bread crumbs
¾ cup canned milk
1 egg, slightly beaten
2 tbsp. chopped onion

Combine ingredients and mix well. Form into patties, using ¼ cup for each pattie. Brown in hot oil. Add to barbecue sauce and simmer for one hour. Serve on buns topped with 1 tsp. of sauce, or serve patties without buns. Makes 12 servings.

Barbecue Sauce

3 tbsp. vinegar
1 cup catsup
½ cup water
2 tbsp. brown sugar
6 tbsp. chopped onion
1 bay leaf
¼-½ tsp. dry mustard

Combine ingredients in saucepan and simmer 5 minutes. Remove bay leaf.

MEATS~CASSEROLES

Swiss Meatballs

1 medium-size onion, chopped
2 tbsp. oil
1 lb. ground beef
¼ cup quick-cooking oatmeal
¼ cup milk
½ tsp. salt
½ cup whole wheat flour
2 beef bouillon cubes
2 cups boiling water

Sauté onion in oil; mix with beef, oatmeal, milk, and salt. Form into walnut-size balls. (Makes about 20.) Place whole wheat flour in a paper bag, add meatballs a few at a time and toss lightly to coat well. Brown meatballs in oil. Place in 1-qt. casserole.

Dissolve bouillon cubes in boiling water and pour over meatballs. Cover and simmer in 325°-350° oven 1 hour and 15 minutes. Keep casserole covered entire time. Can be made in advance and reheated in oven.

Hamburger Roll-Ups

1½ lbs. ground beef
1 cup canned milk
1½ tsp. salt
½ recipe Poultry Stuffing (Dry)
¼ cup catsup
1 can cream of mushroom soup
1 tsp. Worcestershire sauce

Mix ground beef, canned milk and salt. Form into 5-6 patties 6" wide on waxed paper. Place ¼ cup stuffing in center and roll up, sealing edges well. Place in casserole. Mix last 3 ingredients and pour over roll-ups. Bake, uncovered in 350° oven 60-75 minutes.

MEATS~CASSEROLES

Tri-Meatloaf

Grind together:
1 lb. hamburger
¼ lb. ground pork
¼ lb. ground veal
¼ lb. salt pork
2 cups tomatoes

2 tsp. salt
1 tsp. celery salt
1 tsp. onion salt
½ tsp. dry mustard
1 tsp. thyme
1 tsp. sage
¼ tsp. pepper
2 tsp. Worcestershire sauce
1½ cups whole wheat bread crumbs
2 eggs

Mix all ingredients and form into large egg-shaped loaf. Place in baking pan, leaving space around loaf. Let stand in refrigerator 1 hour for meat to absorb seasonings. Pour water in pan to depth of ½". Bake at 350° 30 minutes, then at 325° for 1 hour. Remove from oven and place on hot platter while making gravy. For gravy add ¼ cup whole wheat flour to hot grease, and stir until smooth. Gradually add 2 cups warm water; boil slowly 5 minutes. Season to taste.

Meat Loaf

1 cup whole wheat bread crumbs
1 cup milk
2 lbs. ground beef
1 onion, chopped
2 tsp. salt
1 tbsp. prepared mustard
½ tsp. sage
2 eggs
2 tbsp. finely cut celery (optional)

MEATS~CASSEROLES

Soak crumbs in milk 10 minutes. Add remaining ingredients and bake 1½-2 hours at 300°-325°. Strips of bacon may be put on bottom of loaf pan and on top of meat loaf. Also ½ can of tomato soup may be poured over top before baking, or catsup or chili sauce. If sausage flavor is desired, use following recipe:

1 lb. hamburger
½ lb. sausage
1 onion, chopped
1 cup whole wheat bread crumbs
1 cup milk
2 eggs
1 tsp. salt

Bake 1½-2 hours at 325°.

Hamburger Stroganoff

½ cup minced onion
1 clove garlic, minced
¼ cup butter
1 lb. ground beef
2 tbsp. whole wheat flour
1 tsp. salt
¼ tsp. pepper
4-oz. can sliced mushrooms, undrained
1 can cream of chicken soup, undiluted
1 cup sour cream
2 tbsp. minced parsley

Sauté onion and garlic in butter over medium heat. Add meat and brown. Add flour, salt, pepper and mushrooms. Cook 5-10 minutes on low heat, covered. Add soup and simmer, uncovered, for 10 minutes. Stir in sour cream. Heat through. Sprinkle with parsley. Serve with noodles.

MEATS~CASSEROLES

Stuffed Meat Loaf

1 medium onion, chopped
¾ cup diced celery
3 tbsp. oil
⅓ cup chopped green pepper (optional)
1 tbsp. salt
2 eggs, beaten
3 cups soft whole wheat bread crumbs
   (crust removed)
½ cup water
2 lbs. ground beef
½ cup tomato juice
2 tbsp. margarine

Cook onion and celery in oil until tender. Combine with green pepper, salt, eggs, bread crumbs, and water. Add ½ of this mixture to ground beef, combining well.

Into greased 2-lb. loaf pan, pat ½ of meat mixture. Cover with crumb mixture, then with rest of meat.

Bake at 350° for 15 minutes. Heat tomato juice and melted margarine together. Pour half over the meat; continue baking for 15 minutes. Pour on remaining juice and complete cooking—1½ hours total.

Spanish Wheat

2-3 tbsp. bacon drippings or butter
1 medium onion, chopped
1 green pepper, diced finely
3 cups cooked whole wheat
1 No. 2½ can tomatoes (1 qt.)
Salt and pepper

Cook onion and green pepper in oil until soft. Add wheat, tomatoes, salt and pepper. Cover and simmer 5-6 hours. (The longer the wheat cooks, the more it absorbs the flavor.) Makes 8 servings.

MEATS~CASSEROLES

Angela's Dutch Meat Loaf

1½ lbs. ground beef
⅔ lb. ground pork or ½ lb. sausage
6 slices stale whole wheat bread
   (top crusts removed)
1½ cups milk
3 eggs, beaten
2 tsp. salt
¼ tsp. pepper
¼ tsp. nutmeg or mace
1 tbsp. instant minced onion

Soak bread and milk together for 10 minutes, and add to beaten eggs. Add meat and seasonings and combine well, handling lightly. Shape into loaf and place in well-buttered 2-qt. casserole dish, 12" x 8". Bake at 400° for ½ hour. Reduce heat to 300° for 1 hour longer, or until loaf is done.

Meanwhile, boil together: 4 medium size potatoes, 4 medium size carrots and one finely chopped onion, in 2 cups water with 2 beef bouillon cubes added. When done, drain and mash (not too fine). Season to taste with salt, pepper, and butter. To serve, spoon around sides of meat loaf.

MEATS~CASSEROLES

Hamburger Cracked Wheat Casserole

1 lb. hamburger
½ onion, chopped
1 tsp. salt
dash pepper
2 cups boiling water
¾ cup cracked wheat (uncooked) or bulgur
1 can tomato soup
½-1 tsp. poultry seasoning

Brown onions and meat in frying pan, using a little more fat if necessary. Add salt and pepper. Pour boiling water over cereal and add to meat. Add soup and poultry seasoning and mix thoroughly. Place in greased casserole, cover and bake 40 minutes at 300°-325°. Uncover, stir and bake, 40 minutes longer.

Chinese Noodle Casserole

2 lbs. ground beef
1 large onion, chopped
¾-1 tsp. salt
pepper
1 tbsp. Worcestershire sauce
1 can cream of mushroom soup
1 can cream of chicken soup
1 can water
½ cup uncooked cracked wheat, coarsely ground
1 can Chinese noodles

Brown meat and onion in frying pan. Add salt, pepper, sauce, soups, water and cracked wheat. Mix and place in large greased casserole. Sprinkle with Chinese noodles. Cover with aluminum foil. Bake in 325° oven 1 hour. Uncover and bake 45 minutes longer. Serves about 8.

Variation:

Brown rice may be used instead of cracked wheat.

MEATS~CASSEROLES

Brown Beef Stew

1 lb. boneless stewing beef or
 2 cups Gluten Stew Cubes
2 tsp. salt
½ cup whole wheat flour
oil
2 cups water
2 potatoes, diced
1 onion, sliced
3 carrots, diced
1 cup green beans, fresh or canned

Cut meat into 1" cubes, sprinkle with salt, roll in flour and brown in oil. Add water and simmer 2-3 hours. Add vegetables and cook until tender. Serve with cole slaw. Note:

Note: Hamburger may be used. Brown; add ¼ cup whole wheat flour, vegetables and water and cook ½ hour. If using Gluten Stew Cubes, dredge in flour, brown in oil. Add vegetables and cook until tender.

Feather dumplings are delicious with this stew. Recipe in Soups, Sauces, and Other Savories.

MEATS~CASSEROLES

Glorified Stew

1 lb. stew meat (lamb, beef, venison) cut in 1" cubes, or
2 cups Gluten Stew Cubes
1 large onion or 8 small pearl onions
½ cup whole wheat flour
¼ cup oil
¼ tsp. marjoram or oregano
1 tbsp. lemon juice
3 bay leaves
1 can chicken rice soup
3 soup cans water
1½ tsp. salt (1 tsp. if gluten is used)
¼ tsp. pepper
2-3 carrots (1 lb.) cut in medium size pieces
2-3 potatoes (1 lb.) cut in medium size pieces

Brown meat (dredged in flour) and onions in oil, in 4-qt. pan. Add other ingredients except carrots and potatoes. Cover and simmer 1½ hours. Add carrots, potatoes and more onions if pearl onions are used. Cook 45 minutes, until vegetables are tender.

Can be cooked (covered) in oven.

Note: when using Gluten Stew Cubes, dredge in flour and brown with onions in oil in 4-qt. pan. Then add vegetables and continue cooking until vegetables are tender.

MEATS~CASSEROLES

Lamb's Fry (Liver)

(Beef, pork, or lamb liver may be used.)

1½ lb. sliced liver, cut in 1½" strips
1 cup whole wheat flour
1 tsp. salt
⅛ tsp. pepper
½ lb. bacon, cubed
4 medium onions, sliced thin

Use heavy, 4-qt. pan. Add oil to 1" depth, and heat to "deep frying" temperature. Add liver that has been coated with mixture of flour, salt and pepper. Cook 5 minutes; lift out with slotted spoon and drain in coarse strainer, and then on paper toweling.

Place onions in hot oil. Stir and cook 5-10 minutes until brown. Lift out and drain.

Cook bacon in oil for 3 minutes. Lift out and drain.

Drain off oil.

Place all ingredients in empty pan. Add 3 cups water, ¾ tsp. Kitchen Bouquet, and ¾-1¼ tsp. salt. Simmer until tender. It will thicken as it cooks. Be careful not to burn. Serve over cooked rice, potatoes or macaroni.

MEATS~CASSEROLES

Liver Patties

1 lb. beef liver
1 medium-size onion
1 slice whole wheat bread,
   ¾" thick, dried very hard
1 tsp. salt
⅛ tsp. pepper
2 tbsp. canned milk
2 eggs, beaten slightly

Force liver, onions and dried bread through food chopper, using medium disc. Add salt, pepper, milk and eggs and mix thoroughly. Mixture will be quite moist. Drop by rounded tbsp. into frying pan containing 3 tbsp. oil. Brown on both sides. Place in casserole. Make gravy in frying pan by adding ¼ cup whole wheat flour to remaining fat. Add 3 cups liquid (water or potato water). Stir until smooth. Season to taste. Pour gravy over patties. Cook in 325° to 350° oven 30 minutes, or return patties to gravy in frying pan and cook over slow heat 30 minutes.

Note: Any kind of liver may be used in this recipe.

MEATS~CASSEROLES

Easy Chicken Casserole

3-3½ lb. stewing chicken
1 carrot
1 stalk celery
½ medium onion, chopped
2 tsp. salt
1 bay leaf
2 tbsp. chopped pimiento
   (optional)

Place in large kettle with 4 cups water. Boil gently 2-2½ hours, until tender. Remove chicken. Cool. Take meat from bones and dice with scissors. Makes 3-3½ cups diced chicken. Make sauce with 2 cups chicken broth and 1 cup rich milk, thickened with a paste made with ¼ cup whole wheat flour and ½ cup milk. Season to taste.

Toss together lightly:
3 cups flaked whole wheat bread
   (crusts removed)
½ tsp. salt
1 medium onion, browned in
½ cup butter
½ tsp. celery salt
1 tsp. sage

Place half of bread crumb mixture in buttered 2-qt. casserole. Add diced chicken and top with rest of crumb mixture. Pour chicken sauce over all. Sprinkle top with mixture of 1 cup whole wheat bread crumbs and ¼ cup margarine. Bake at 325°-350° for 1¼-1½ hours.

MEATS ~ CASSEROLES

Chicken Paprika

4-5 lb. chicken
1 tsp. salt
½ tsp. pepper
½ cup whole wheat flour
2 tbsp. paprika
¼ cup onion flakes
3 tbsp. whole wheat flour
1 cup milk
¼ cup oil
2 cups boiling water

Clean chicken and cut into serving pieces. (Use wing tips, back and neck for chicken soup.) Sprinkle with salt and pepper. Flour lightly (shake off excess flour). Brown on all sides in hot oil. Sprinkle with paprika. Add onion flakes and water. Cover; simmer 1½-2 hours, until tender. Remove chicken to serving dish. Blend 3 tbsp. flour and milk; add to liquid in pan. Cook until thickened. Pour over chicken. Makes 6 servings.

Delicious Well-Done Chicken

Cut chicken into serving pieces. Dip in milk (1 cup milk plus ¼ cup canned milk). Sprinkle with salt. Dip in whole wheat flour. Brown in frying pan, adding a little more salt; use plenty of oil.

Place browned chicken in Dutch oven or casserole. Add 1 cup water to frying pan and stir to remove all brown. Giblet water may be used. Season if necessary. Add liquid to chicken. Cover and cook at 350° for ½ hour, then reduce heat to 300° for 1½ hours.

MEATS~CASSEROLES

Poultry Dressing

(Good even cooked alone)

½ cup onion, finely chopped
1 cup celery, finely chopped
1 cup butter or margarine
1 tsp. salt
¼ tsp. pepper
1 tbsp. poultry seasoning
1 lb. whole wheat bread crumbs
1½ cups boiling water or
   giblet liquid
giblets ground fine

Brown onion and celery in butter. Mix dry ingredients with bread crumbs. Add liquid, ground giblets, onion and celery.

If cooking alone, place in buttered casserole. Cover and bake at 325°-350° for 1-1½ hours. Uncover long enough to brown lightly.

Poultry Stuffing (Moist)

½ cup butter or margarine
½ cup minced onion
½ cup diced celery, or
   1 tsp. celery salt
6 cups soft whole wheat bread
   crumbs, crusts removed
1 tsp. salt
1 tsp. sage
2 eggs, beaten
giblet liquid or water to moisten
giblets, ground or chopped,
   if desired

Cook onion and celery in butter. Combine bread crumbs, salt, sage, onion and celery. Add beaten eggs and liquid to moisten.

117

MEATS ~ CASSEROLES

Poultry Stuffing (Dry)

3 tbsp. butter
1 medium onion, chopped, or
   2 tbsp. dry minced onion
¼ cup diced celery, or
   ½ tsp. celery salt
2 cups soft whole wheat bread
   crumbs, crusts removed
½ tsp. salt
½ tsp. sage

Cook onion and celery in butter. Combine and blend all ingredients.

French Harvest Chicken Casserole

(A favorite of French farmers, served as a delicacy after the wheat harvest—a perfect and easy casserole dish.)

Cut 3-lb. fryer chicken into individual portions. Make broth of giblets, neck, wing tips, back, plus 1 sliced carrot, 1 sliced onion, 1 bay leaf, ¼ tsp. thyme, and 4 cups water. Add ¾ tsp. salt, ⅛ tsp. pepper, and boil for 1½-2 hours. Rub chicken with mixture of 3 tbsp. soy sauce and 1 tbsp. honey. Sprinkle with salt and fry in 4-6 tbsp. oil until golden brown. Place in large casserole and cover with mixture of 1 cup coarse cracked wheat and ½ tsp. basil. Add 3 cups strained giblet broth. Cover and bake at 350° for 1½-2 hours, adding more liquid if necessary. Keep covered until ready to serve.

Note: If cracked wheat is too fine, sieve some of finer particles out. Use the chicken from broth for creamed chicken or chicken salad. Use scissors to dice.

MEATS~CASSEROLES

Chicken Pie

(15 *individual pies*)

3½-4½ lb. chicken or turkey
6 cups water
½ cup diced celery, or
   handful of celery tops
1 large bay leaf
1 tbsp. salt
¼ tsp. pepper
½ cup whole wheat flour
1 cup milk
¼ cup butter
½ cup chopped onions
1 cup diced celery
2 cups diced carrots
2 cups diced potatoes
1 pkg. frozen peas
1½ tsp. salt

Combine chicken or turkey, water, celery, bay leaf, salt and pepper in large kettle. Cover and simmer 2 hours, until meat comes off bones easily. Strain off stock. Cool chicken and cut into bite size pieces, using scissors. (Should have at least 3 cups.)

Heat 4 cups stock. (If short, add top milk to make up difference.)

Make thickening of ½ cup whole wheat flour and 1 cup milk. Add to heated stock and cook until thickened. Remove from heat and add meat.

Brown onion in ¼ cup butter until tender. Cook carrots and celery until tender. When about half done, add diced potatoes and frozen peas, and finish cooking. Stir in salt and browned onions and add to chicken mixture. Fill each individual pie tin with about ¾ cup of mixture. Place a round of pastry on top of each, using a No. 2 can as cutter. Cut 3 slits in top of each pastry round. (This top may be a baking powder biscuit.) Bake at 425° for 30-35 minutes.

Pies may be frozen before baking. Put frozen pie into oven without thawing. Allow 15-20 minutes extra time for baking. Reduce heat to 350° last 15 minutes.

MEATS~CASSEROLES

Baked Chicken Squares

3 cups cubed, cooked chicken
   (1 large stewing chicken)
2 cups soft whole wheat bread crumbs
1 cup cooked rice
2 tbsp. minced pimiento
1½ tsp. salt
2 cups chicken broth
1 cup milk
4 eggs, well beaten
Chicken-Mushroom Sauce (recipe below)

Layer chicken, bread crumbs, rice, pimiento, and salt in 12" x 8" baking pan or 2-qt. oblong casserole.

Mix broth and milk. Stir in beaten eggs. Pour over chicken mixture. Bake at 325° about 50 minutes, until set. Cut into squares and serve with hot Chicken-Mushroom Sauce.

Chicken-Mushroom Sauce

¼ cup margarine
6 tbsp. whole wheat flour
2 cups chicken broth
¼ cup canned milk
4-oz. can mushrooms, drained
1 tsp. (rounded) minced parsley
½ tsp. lemon juice
½ tsp. salt

Melt butter in saucepan. Blend in flour. Gradually add broth and canned milk. Cook until thickened. Stir in mushrooms parsley, lemon juice and salt.

MEATS~CASSEROLES

Fish

Any fish suitable for frying or baking may be rolled in whole wheat flour or seasoned flour (see earlier in this section). Then fry or bake as usual.

Fillet of Fish

4 fillets of sole, halibut or salmon
½ cup whole wheat flour
⅓ cup melted butter or margarine
½ tsp. salt
¼ tsp. dry mustard
¼ cup tartar sauce
paprika
pepper

Dust fillets lightly with flour. Mix butter, salt, mustard and pepper. Brush top of fillets, using about ⅓ of seasoned butter. Spread with tartar sauce (about 1 tbsp. to each fillet). Sprinkle with paprika. Place on preheated broiler rack and broil 2-3 inches from heat 5-8 minutes. Baste once with seasoned butter. Turn once. Serve hot.

MEATS ~ CASSEROLES

Salmon Loaf

1 1-lb. can salmon
1 cup whole wheat bread crumbs
¾ tsp. salt
1 cup milk
3-4 hard-boiled eggs
butter

Mix ingredients well. Place in well-greased loaf pan or individual baking dishes and dot with butter. Bake in pan of water 30-45 minutes at 325°-350°. Serve with egg white sauce as follows:

2 cups milk
¼ cup whole wheat flour
½ tsp. salt
2 hard boiled eggs, chopped
4 tbsp. butter
2 tbsp. minced parsley

Cook as for White Sauce and add eggs.

Sea Food Casserole

2½ lbs. halibut or salmon

Steam with 4 slices onion and 2 bay leaves until tender, about 20 minutes. Cut into pieces and place in buttered, 3-qt. oblong casserole. Trim crusts from 6 slices whole wheat bread; cube and place on top of fish. Pour over fish and cubed bread the following sauce:

¼ lb. butter or margarine
½ cup whole wheat flour
1 tsp. dry mustard
4 cups milk

Cook until thickened. Add 1-2 cups grated cheese.

Sprinkle top with mixture of 1 cup whole wheat bread crumbs and ¼ cup butter or margarine. Bake at 350° for 30-45 minutes.

Stuffed Halibut Steaks

4 halibut steaks
sprinkle of salt
1 cup cooked rice
1 cup soft whole wheat bread crumbs (crusts removed)
1/3 cup chopped celery
1/3 cup chopped onion
2 tbsp. chopped parsley
1 tsp. curry powder
1/2 tsp. celery seed
1 tsp. salt
2 tbsp. melted butter
1/4 cup melted butter
2 tbsp. chopped parsley
2 tsp. lemon juice

Heat oven to 350°. Butter shallow baking dish large enough to hold 2 halibut steaks. Sprinkle all steaks lightly with salt. Place 2 in baking dish.

Combine rice, bread crumbs, celery, onion, 2 tbsp. parsley, curry powder, celery seed, 1 tsp. salt and 2 tbsp. butter. Top steaks in dish with this dressing. Put remaining 2 steaks on top of dressing and fasten steaks with tooth picks.

Combine remaining 1/4 cup butter, 2 tbsp. parsley and lemon juice, and pour over steaks. Bake about 30 minutes, until steaks flake easily with fork.

Serves 4. Perch or other fish fillets may be used.

MEATS~CASSEROLES

Tuna Fish Loaf with Celery-Olive Sauce

2 eggs, beaten
1 cup canned milk
2 tbsp. melted butter
½ tsp. salt
¼ tsp. pepper
2 tbsp. chopped pimiento
2 tbsp. chopped parsley
2 cans tuna fish
1 cup soft whole wheat bread crumbs (crusts removed)

Combine ingredients in order given. Bake in well-greased 1-qt. casserole or loaf pan (pyrex) at 325°-350° for 45 minutes. Serve with following sauce:

1 can cream of celery soup
¼ cup canned milk
¼ cup sliced ripe olives

Economical Ham Loaf

6 tbsp. uncooked rice
1½ cups milk
½ cup ground whole wheat bread crumbs
¾ lb. ground ham
1½ lbs. ground beef
2 eggs, beaten
¾-1 tsp. salt (depending on how salty the ham is)

Cook rice in 1 cup cold water with ¼ tsp. salt. Mix milk and bread crumbs and let stand while rice is cooking. Combine meat, crumbs, rice, eggs and salt. Mix and press into greased loaf pan, 9" x 5" x 3".

Bake at 350° for 45 minutes, then at 300° for 45 minutes more.

Serve with a creamed vegetable.

MEATS~CASSEROLES

Tuna Fish Roll-Ups

2 cups *sifted* whole wheat flour
4 tsp. baking powder
¾ tsp. salt
⅓ cup oil
⅔ cup milk (about)

Sift dry ingredients together twice. Add liquids and stir with fork until mixture cleans sides of bowl and forms ball. Roll on floured board into oblong sheet. Cut into 9 squares. Place 2 tbsp. tuna filling on each square. Roll up and bake 15 minutes at 400°-425°. Serve with hot sauce made by adding ⅓ cup milk to either celery, mushroom or chicken soup. 2 tbsp. chopped parsley may be added, also paprika.

Note: Batter may be made from Wheatquick Mix No. 1.

Tuna Filling:

1 can tuna fish (flaked)
½ cup celery, finely chopped
1 egg, unbeaten
Mix together well.

MEATS~CASSEROLES

Tamale Pie

1 lb. hamburger
1 large onion
2 tbsp. oil
1 can tomato soup
1 tsp. salt
dash of pepper
1-2 tsp. chili powder
¾ cup fresh or canned corn

Brown hamburger in oil. Add all other ingredients and cook over slow heat while mixing the topping.

Topping:

⅓ cup whole wheat flour
½ tsp. salt
2 tsp. baking powder
½ cup yellow corn meal
1 egg, beaten
2 tbsp. oil
¾ cup milk

For topping, sift together all dry ingredients. Combine egg, oil and milk. Add to dry ingredients and blend.

Place hamburger mixture in 2-qt. casserole. Cover with topping and bake at 400° for 25 minutes.

MEATS~CASSEROLES

Beef and Potato Casserole

½ cup whole wheat flour
1 lb. stewing beef or 2 cups
   Gluten Stew Cubes (see recipe)
3 tsp. oil
3 cups water
2 onions, chopped
1 tsp. Worcestershire sauce
2 tsp. salt
dash of pepper
2 large potatoes

Put flour in clean paper bag. Drop in pieces of meat and shake well until all water is taken up. (If meat seems dry, sprinkle first with water, then add to flour in paper sack and proceed.) Thoroughly brown floured meat in hot oil. Place in casserole. Add 3 cups water to frying pan and boil to dissolve browned flour and juices. Pour this over meat, add onion, Worcestershire sauce, salt and pepper. Cover and simmer for two hours. Start oven at 350°, then turn down to 325°. Rich gravy thickens and colors itself while cooking. During last hour, add potatoes cut in eighths.

Veal, lamb, pork and venison are delicious cooked this way.

Corned Beef Casserole

6 oz. noodles, cooked and drained
1 can mushroom soup
¾ soup can of milk
12-oz. can corned beef, chilled and
   cut into cubes
½ cup finely chopped onions, or
   1 tsp. instant minced onion
1 cup whole wheat bread crumbs
¼ cup margarine

Combine noodles, mushroom soup, milk, corned beef and onions. Place in 2-qt. oblong buttered casserole. Blend bread crumbs and margarine and spread over other ingredients. Bake at 350° for 45 minutes.

MEATS~CASSEROLES

Corned Beef Loaf

2 eggs, beaten
1 cup milk
1 cup soft whole wheat bread crumbs (crust removed)
1 tbsp. prepared mustard
1 tsp. instant minced onion
¼ green pepper (optional)
12-oz. can corned beef (room temp.)

Beat eggs; add milk, bread crumbs, and seasonings. Stir in corned beef that has been flaked or shredded. Blend well and place in greased 1½-qt. loaf pan. Dot with butter and let stand at least ½ hour before baking. Bake at 350° for 45 minutes. Let stand 5-10 minutes before cutting.

Note: This loaf may be mixed in the morning and set in refrigerator until time for baking.

Armenian Cabbage Rolls

1 medium size head cabbage
1 lb. ground lamb or beef
2 cups coarse cracked wheat
1½ tsp. salt
⅛ tsp. pepper
1 qt. tomato juice or canned tomatoes (more or less)

Separate cabbage leaves and place in boiling water about 5 minutes, until limp. Combine meat, cracked wheat, salt and pepper and mix well. Roll about 2 level tbsp. meat mixture in each cabbage leaf. If leaves are too large, divide in two. Wrap tightly and lay one on top of the other in large kettle. Place rack or slab of marble on bottom of kettle so rolls will not rest on heat. Almost cover rolls with tomato juice or canned tomatoes and boil about 1 hour until meat mixture is well done. Pour off juice and keep it hot to serve with rolls. Do not allow rolls to stand in juice after they are cooked.

Crab Casserole

1 cup milk
1 cup mayonnaise
1½ cups soft whole wheat bread crumbs (crusts removed)
1 can crab, flaked (1 cup)
1 tbsp. parsley
1 tsp. chopped onion
¼ tsp. salt
6 hard-boiled eggs, coarsely chopped
1 cup dry whole wheat bread crumbs
2 tbsp. butter

Mix milk and mayonnaise. Toss in bread crumbs, crab, and other ingredients (except dry bread crumbs and butter). Mix lightly and place in buttered 1½-qt. casserole. Mix dry bread crumbs and butter, and place over top. Bake at 350° for 45 minutes.

Onion-Wheat Casserole

1 lb. ground beef
1 large onion, diced
2 cups diced celery
½ tsp. salt
dash of pepper
1 can onion soup
½ can water
¾ cup cracked wheat

Partially brown meat in skillet; add chopped onion, celery, salt and pepper, and continue to brown. Add soup, water and cracked wheat. Pour into large shallow casserole dish and bake at 350° for 1½ hours. 6-8 servings.

MEATS~CASSEROLES

Asparagus and Ham Au Gratin

2 cups soft whole wheat bread crumbs (crusts removed)
¾ cup grated cheese
¼ cup melted butter
no. 2 can asparagus (2½ cups)
2 tbsp. butter
2 tbsp. minced onion
3 tbsp. whole wheat flour
1 tsp. salt
¼ tsp. pepper
1 cup milk
1 cup diced, cooked ham

Mix bread crumbs, cheese and melted butter. Place ½ of this mixture in buttered 2-qt. casserole. Arrange asparagus over this. Brown onion in 2 tbsp. butter. Blend in flour, salt and pepper. Remove from heat and add milk slowly. Return to heat and cook until thickened, stirring constantly to prevent lumping and burning. Blend in ham. Pour over asparagus and top with remaining crumb mixture. Bake at 350° for 25-30 minutes. Makes 4-6 servings.

Cracked Wheat-Lentil Casserole

1 cup lentils, washed well
1 cup coarse cracked wheat
4 cups tomato juice
1 lb. ground beef or lamb
1 medium onion, chopped
1½ tsp. salt
½-1 tsp. chili powder
¼ tsp. pepper
¼ tsp. oregano
2 cups tomato juice or tomatoes

Place lentils, cracked wheat, and 4 cups tomato juice in 2-qt. casserole and soak overnight, or 6 hours. Place covered casserole in 300° oven and cook for 3 hours. Stir often to prevent sticking.

Brown meat and onion together. Add salt, chili powder, pepper, oregano and tomato juice. Combine with casserole mixture and bake 1 hour, leaving lid off last ½ hour. Add more juice or a little water if mixture seems dry. This makes a very nutritious main course to serve with a vegetable and a tossed salad.

MEATS~CASSEROLES

Italian Macaroni Loaf

1 cup macaroni or spaghetti
1½ cups scalded milk
1 cup soft whole wheat bread crumbs (crusts removed)
¼ cup melted butter
1 pimiento, chopped
1 tbsp. parsley
1 tbsp. chopped onion
1½ cups grated cheese
¼ tsp. salt
⅛ tsp. pepper
¼ tsp. paprika
3 eggs, well beaten

Cook macaroni in salted water, drain and rinse with cold water.

Pour scalded milk over bread crumbs. Add butter, pimiento, parsley, onion, cheese and seasonings. Stir in well-beaten eggs.

Place macaroni in well-buttered loaf pan, 9" x 5" x 3", and pour milk and cheese mixture over it. Bake at 325°-350° about 50 minutes, until loaf is firm and will hold its shape when turned out on platter. Serve with Mushroom Sauce.

Mushroom Sauce

1 tbsp. butter
¼ cup whole wheat flour
¼ tsp. salt
⅛ tsp. pepper
⅛ tsp. paprika
1½ cups milk
½ cup liquid from mushrooms
4-oz. can mushrooms, drained

Melt butter; blend in whole wheat flour and seasonings. Add milk and mushroom liquid gradually, stirring until thickened. Add mushrooms. May use with any recipe calling for creamed sauce.

VEGETABLES

Western Celery Casserole

¾ cup whole wheat bread crumbs
¼ cup slivered almonds (optional)
¼ cup melted butter
4 *heaping* cups celery, cut in
    1" pieces
1 can sliced mushrooms
1 can water chestnuts, sliced
    thin (optional)
1 small can sliced pimiento
2 cans cream of chicken soup, or
    2 cups Medium White Sauce
½ soup can of milk

Brown bread crumbs and almonds in butter and set aside for topping. Cook celery in slightly salted boiling water about 5 minutes. Drain. Place in buttered, oblong 2-qt. casserole. Add mushrooms, chestnuts and pimiento on top of celery. Cover with soup and milk mixed. Sprinkle with buttered crumbs and almonds. Bake at 350°-375° for 45 minutes. This is good served with chicken or ham.

Asparagus and Egg Casserole

1 lb. asparagus, cut in 1" pieces
2 hard-cooked eggs
2 cups Medium White Sauce
1 cup whole wheat bread crumbs
6 tbsp. butter

Cook asparagus until tender; place in well-buttered 1-qt. casserole. Slice eggs on top and add white sauce. Cover with buttered bread crumbs. Bake at 350° 35-40 minutes.

Variation:

Canned asparagus, drained, may be substituted for fresh asparagus.

Dutch Snap Beans

2 slices bacon, diced
4 tbsp. diced onion
2 tbsp. whole wheat flour
1 cup juice from beans
1/8 tsp. pepper
1 tbsp. lemon juice
4 cups cooked snap beans,
    (2 no. 2 cans)

Brown bacon in skillet and add onion and brown lightly. Add flour, hot bean juice and pepper. Cook, stirring constantly until smooth and thickened. Add lemon juice and beans. Boil 10 minutes. Serve.

Cabbage Timbale

3 cups shredded cabbage
1 cup water
3 eggs
1 cup milk
2 tbsp. whole wheat flour
1 tsp. salt
1 tsp. raw sugar
1 cup soft whole wheat bread crumbs
3 tbsp. melted butter
1/2 tbsp. onion, finely chopped

Boil cabbage in 1 cup water 5 minutes. Drain. Beat eggs slightly and add milk. Mix flour, salt and sugar and add to egg mixture. Add cabbage and remaining ingredients. Mix and pour into buttered casserole. Place in pan of water. Bake at 325°-350° 30 minutes, or until knife comes out clean. If using canned milk, dilute it with water from boiled cabbage.

VEGETABLES

Baked Corn and Tomatoes

2 cups whole kernel corn
2 cups tomatoes
1 tsp. salt
1/8 tsp. pepper
1 tsp. raw sugar
1 cup soft whole wheat bread crumbs
3 tbsp. butter

Mix corn, tomatoes, salt, pepper, sugar and pour into greased baking dish. Top with buttered bread crumbs. Bake at 350° 30 minutes.

Variation:

1. A 1-lb. can stewed tomatoes may be substituted for tomatoes, in which case eliminate salt, pepper and sugar.

2. 1/2 lb. zucchini may be added.

Scalloped Tomatoes

3/4-1 lb. link sausages
2 medium size onions, chopped
4 slices whole wheat bread, cubed
no. 2 1/2 can tomatoes (3 1/2 cups)
1 tsp. salt

Brown sausages in frying pan; remove to casserole. Pour off half of fat and brown onions, adding cubed bread just before onions are thoroughly browned. Place half of seasoned tomatoes over sausages in casserole. Layer half of onion and bread cube mixture, then remaining tomatoes, and top with balance of onions and bread cubes. Bake at 350° 45-60 minutes, reducing heat to 325° last 1/2 hour.

Note: Chopped bacon, wieners or vienna sausages may be substituted for sausages. When using wieners or vienna sausages, brown in bacon drippings or oil sufficient for onions and bread cubes. This is delicious without meat, and was a favorite pioneer recipe.

Scalloped Corn

1 can cream style corn
2/3 cup milk
1/4 tsp. salt
dash pepper
2 tbsp. butter
2 cups whole wheat bread crumbs

Mix corn, milk and seasonings. Mix crumbs and butter. Alternate the two mixtures in a buttered baking dish with crumbs on top. Bake at 350° for 30 minutes.

Zucchini Squash Casserole

1 lb. zucchini squash (medium size)
1 cup medium white sauce
3/4 cup nippy cheese
1/4 tsp. mustard
dash pepper
1/2 tsp. Worcestershire sauce
1/2 cup buttered whole wheat bread crumbs

Wash squash but do not peel. Cut in 1/2" slices and cook in salted boiling water (1/2 tsp. salt) until barely tender. Melt cheese in white sauce. Add mustard, pepper and Worcestershire sauce. Place squash in casserole and cover with white sauce mixture. Top with 1/2 cup whole wheat bread crumbs. Bake at 325°-350° for 30 minutes. Serves 4.

VEGETABLES

Potatoes Au Gratin

4-6 unpeeled potatoes
2 cups medium white sauce
½ lb. grated cheese
1 tsp. grated onion *or*
   ¼ tsp. onion salt
½ cup whole wheat bread crumbs

Boil potatoes in salted water. Cool, peel and cut or cube in small pieces. Add white sauce and ¼ lb. grated cheese and onion or onion salt. Add more salt if necessary. Place in baking dish. Sprinkle crumbs and remaining cheese on top. Bake at 325°-350° for 30 minutes or until cheese is melted and slightly browned. Serves 6.

Baked Zucchini Squash (Stuffed)

1 lb. zucchini squash (medium size)
¾ cup grated nippy cheese
¾ cup whole wheat bread crumbs
1 cup medium white sauce
sprinkle of salt
dash of pepper

Wash squash but do not peel. Cook in boiling, salted water (½ tsp. salt) until barely tender. Drain, cool and cut lengthwise. Scoop out center of squash. Add remaining ingredients to pulp. Season to taste. Fill in center of squash. Dot with butter. Place on baking sheet and bake at 325°-350° for 30 minutes.

SOUPS, SAUCES, SAVORIES

White Sauce

Thin:

1 cup milk
1 tbsp. whole wheat flour
1 tbsp. fat
¼ tsp. salt
dash pepper

Medium:

1 cup milk
2 tbsp. whole wheat flour
2 tbsp. fat
¼ tsp. salt
dash pepper

Thick:

1 cup milk
3 tbsp. whole wheat flour
2 tbsp. fat
¼ tsp. salt
dash pepper

Fat may be butter, meat drippings or oil. The liquid may be cream, milk, water or meat stock. To use dry skim milk, mix ¾ cup dried milk with 2 cups water in blender or with egg beater. Pour into quart measure and fill with water.

The seasonings may be combinations of celery salt, onion salt, mustard, cloves, bay leaf, sugar, flavoring extracts, grated cheese etc.

Methods:

1. Melt fat in saucepan. Add flour salt and pepper. Stir until smooth. Remove from heat while adding hot liquid. Stir constantly, cooking until mixture thickens. Boil 2 minutes. If made in double boiler, cook 10-15 minutes.

SOUPS, SAUCES, SAVORIES

2. Mix flour, salt and pepper to smooth paste with a little cold liquid. Use a small jar with tight lid to save time and shake until smooth. Blend with hot liquid. Boil 2 minutes. Add fat as sauce is removed from heat. If made in double boiler, cook 10-15 minutes.

3. Brown sauce for gravy is made by browning the flour in the fat very slowly before adding the liquid.

Method 2 is especially adaptable to making sauce in large quantities.

Feather Dumplings

2 cups *sifted* whole wheat flour
1 tsp. salt
4 tsp. baking powder
⅛ tsp. pepper
⅔ cup milk
1 egg, beaten well
3 tbsp. oil

Sift dry ingredients together twice. Add milk, egg, and oil. Mix just until blended. Drop by teaspoon into boiling liquid. Cover and cook 18 minutes. (Can be used in any stew.)

Note: These are delicious cooked with boiling plums to make "plum dumplings." Add ¼ cup sweetening to dry ingredients.

SOUPS, SAUCES, SAVORIES

Whole Wheat Herb Dumplings

1½ cups *sifted* whole wheat flour
3 tsp. baking powder
½ tsp. salt
⅛ tsp. poultry seasoning
2 tbsp. parsley
1 egg, beaten
¾ cup milk

Combine dry ingredients. Add beaten egg and milk. Stir with fork, just to blend. Drop by teaspoonfuls on top of stew. Cook, covered, 15 minutes. Uncover, and cook 5 minutes more.

Whole Wheat Batter (Croquettes or Patties)

1 cup *sifted* whole wheat flour
½ tsp. salt
2 tsp. baking powder
1 egg, beaten
½ cup milk
2 cups ground cooked meat, canned fish or mashed vegetables

This batter is suitable for making Salmon Patties, Tuna Patties, Parsnip Fritters, or any vegetable, meat or fish patty, or croquette. Combine all ingredients. Shape into patties and brown in hot oil. When making croquettes, roll each portion in fine bread crumbs and brown in oil.

SOUPS, SAUCES, SAVORIES

Salad Croutons

½ garlic clove, cut fine
½ cup salad oil (corn, peanut or olive)
1 cup ½" diced bread cubes (stale bread, crusts removed)

Combine chopped garlic with salad oil. Cover tightly and refrigerate 1 hour. Place 2 tbsp. garlic mixture in medium size skillet. Sauté bread cubes until brown on all sides. Set aside to be added to tossed salad.

Note: For Soup Croutons, cut buttered, stale bread in 1" cubes and toast in 350° oven 10 minutes, stirring occasionally.

Salad Dressing:

To remaining garlic mixture in jar, add:
¾ tsp. salt
¼ tsp. dry mustard
¼ tsp. freshly ground black pepper
1½ tsp. Worcestershire sauce

Shake vigorously and refrigerate. Use on any tossed salad.

Economical Potato Soup

8 medium size potatoes, peeled and sliced
2 medium size onions, finely cut
2 qts. water
1 cup canned milk
2 tbsp. butter or margarine
salt and pepper
1 tbsp. chopped chives or parsley

Cook potatoes and onions in 2 qts. water, covered, 45 minutes. Mash well. Stir in milk, butter and seasonings. Simmer 15 minutes. Do not boil. Sprinkle with chives or parsley and serve with Soup Croutons (see Salad Croutons).

SOUPS, SAUCES, SAVORIES

Baked Omelet

4 eggs
1 cup milk
3 tbsp. whole wheat flour
¼ tsp. salt
½ cup grated cheese
1 slice whole wheat bread, cubed
  (crust removed)

Preheat oven to 450°. Melt 2 tbsp. margarine in 1-qt. casserole. Beat eggs; add milk, flour and salt. Add cheese and bread cubes. (Ham, bacon or parsley may be added.) Place in casserole and bake in hot oven for 10 minutes. Reduce to 350° and continue to bake 20 minutes, or until knife inserted in center comes out clean.

Ham and Cheese Fondue

6 slices buttered whole wheat bread
  (crusts removed)
6 slices cheddar cheese
3 slices boiled ham
1 tbsp. prepared mustard
3 eggs, slightly beaten
2 cups milk
1 tsp. salt
¼ tsp. pepper

Top 3 slices of bread with 1 slice cheese, 1 slice ham, 1 slice cheese. Spread 3 remaining slices of bread with mustard, and place on top to make sandwich.
Cut each sandwich into 4 squares and place in well-buttered 2-qt. oblong baking dish. Beat eggs; add milk, salt and pepper. Pour over bread squares. Set baking dish in pan of hot water and bake at 325° for 45 minutes or until knife comes out clean. Let stand 10 minutes before serving. Serve with any good salad.

SOUPS, SAUCES, SAVORIES

Split Pea Soup

2 cups green split peas
2 qts. cold water
2 medium-size onions
4 large stalks celery
   (including tops)
2 medium size potatoes
1 qt. milk (fresh or canned)
4 tsp. salt
   pepper

Cook in 4-qt. pan, or use deep well in electric range, or crockpot.

Split peas may be soaked overnight in 2 qts. water, in which case be sure to cook them in the same water. Alternatively, omit soaking and allow longer cooking time. Cook together the peas, finely cut onions, celery and potatoes until tender. Put through strainer or use egg beater to blend. Add seasonings and milk.

Serve with croutons made from buttered whole wheat bread, cubed and browned in 350° oven about 10 minutes.

Note: This soup, without milk, can be frozen and milk added later. See Salad Croutons, this section.

Variations:

1. Omit potatoes. When peas are tender, put through strainer. Make a white sauce of 4 tbsp. butter or bacon fat, 4 tbsp. whole wheat flour and 1 qt. milk. Combine soup, white sauce and seasonings.

2. May be served with wieners, sliced thin and added just before servings. Finely chopped bacon, fried to a delicate brown, may be added just before serving.

SOUPS, SAUCES, SAVORIES

Danish Soup

6 medium carrots, cubed
4 medium potatoes, cubed
1 medium onion, chopped
2 sticks celery, cut
2 tsp. salt
2 cups tomatoes or juice
1 lb. hamburger
1 tsp. salt
¼ tsp. pepper
¼ tsp. sage
1 egg (optional)
½ slice whole wheat bread
¼ cup milk
1 tbsp. whole wheat flour
1½ cups boiling water
2 bouillon cubes

Cook vegetables in 2 qts. salted water until tender. Add tomatoes. Combine meat, salt, pepper, sage, egg, bread, milk and flour. Form into marble-size balls. Cook in 1½ cups boiling water 10 minutes, with bouillon cubes added. Pour liquid and meat balls over cooked vegetables. Simmer 10 minutes. Add minced parsley. Makes 4 qts.

SOUPS, SAUCES, SAVORIES

Chili Beef on Buns

1 onion, chopped
2 tbsp. oil
1 lb. ground beef
½ tsp. salt
½ tsp. chili powder
1 can tomato soup
⅔ cup grated cheese

Brown onion in oil; add meat and brown slightly. Add salt, chili powder and tomato soup. Simmer 30 minutes. Remove from heat and *cool*. Blend in cheese. Split whole wheat hamburger buns and spread mixture on each half bun. Place under broiler until cheese melts and buns are slightly browned (3-5 minutes). Serve hot.

Note: Double recipe is ample for 40 bun halves. ¾ lb. cheese needed for double recipe. Very good served with fruit salad. Any leftover meat mixture may be frozen.

Nourishing Sandwich Filling

Blend together:

½ cup peanut butter
½ cup wheat germ
½ cup honey
3 tbsp. butter

Spread on whole wheat bread.

SOUPS, SAUCES, SAVORIES

Hot Tuna Sandwich

6½-oz. can drained, flaked tuna
¼ lb. diced American cheese
3 hard cooked eggs, chopped
3 tbsp. well-drained pickle relish
2 tbsp. chopped onion
½ cup mayonnaise
3 tbsp. sliced pimiento-stuffed
 olives, or ripe olives

Spread mixture on 6 buttered hamburger bun halves. Top with remaining bun halves. Wrap each bun in aluminum foil. Place in preheated 400° oven 15 minutes. Serves 6. (Make buns with Superior Quick Whole Wheat Bread recipe.)

COOKIES

(Do not crowd on cookie sheet and do not overbake any refrigerator cookie.)

Refrigerator Cookies

3 cups *sifted* whole wheat flour
½ tsp. salt
1 cup butter or margarine
2 cups raw or brown sugar
2 eggs, beaten
½ tsp. salt
1 tsp. soda, dissolved in
1 tbsp. hot water
1 cup nuts or coconut

Sift flour and salt together twice. Cream butter and sugar together. Add eggs, then dissolved soda with flour. Add nuts. Form into 2 rolls. Wrap in waxed paper. Refrigerate overnight. Slice thin and bake 8-10 minutes at 350°-375°.

Note: Spice cookies may be made from this recipe by adding 1 tsp. cinnamon and ½ tsp. nutmeg.

Oatmeal Refrigerator Cookies

1½ cups *sifted* whole wheat flour
1 tsp. salt
1 tsp. soda
1 cup margarine or butter
2 cups raw or brown sugar
2 eggs, well beaten
1 tsp. vanilla
3 cups oatmeal
½ cup chopped nuts

Sift together, twice, the flour, salt and soda. Cream butter, sugar, eggs and vanilla. Add sifted flour, oatmeal and nuts and blend well. Shape into 2 rolls. Wrap in waxed paper and refrigerate overnight. Slice ¼" thick. Bake 8-10 minutes at 350°-375°.

Date Pinwheel Cookies

Filling:

2¼ cups chopped dates (1 lb.)
½ cup raw or brown sugar
1 cup water
1 cup chopped nuts

Cook dates, sugar and water until thick. Add nuts and chill.

Dough:

1 cup butter or margarine
2 cups raw or brown sugar
3 eggs, well beaten
4 cups *sifted* whole wheat flour
½ tsp. salt
½ tsp. soda

Sift together, twice, the flour, salt and soda. Cream butter and sugar and add well-beaten eggs. Add dry ingredients and blend well. Chill. Roll dough ¼" thick on waxed paper and spread with filling. Roll like a jelly roll. Wrap in waxed paper. Chill in refrigerator at least 3 hours or overnight. Slice ¼" thick. Bake 10-12 minutes at 375°-400°.

Variation: Raisins may be substituted for dates. Use same amount.

COOKIES

Date-Nut Refrigerator Cookies

3½ cups *sifted* whole wheat flour
½ tsp. baking powder
¾ tsp. salt
2 cups raw or brown sugar
1 cup butter or margarine
2 eggs, well beaten
1 tsp. soda, dissolved in
2 tbsp. water
1 lb. dates, cut in pieces with scissors
1 cup chopped nuts and/or 1 cup coconut

Sift together, twice, the flour, baking powder and salt. Cream butter and sugar. Add eggs, then soda and water. Add dry ingredients and stir in nuts and dates. Form into rolls, wrap in waxed paper and refrigerate overnight. Cut in ¼" slices and bake 8-10 minutes at 350°-375°. If rolls are not too fat, yield is about 150 cookies.

Variation: Raisins may be substituted for dates, if desired.

Orange Roll-Out Cookies

3 cups *sifted* whole wheat flour
½ tsp. salt
2 tsp. baking powder
⅔ cup margarine or butter
1¼ cup raw or brown sugar
2 eggs, beaten
grated rind of 1 orange
2-3 tbsp. orange juice

Sift together, twice, the flour, salt and baking powder. Cream margarine and sugar, add beaten eggs and mix well. Add sifted dry ingredients and orange rind and juice. Mix thoroughly. Roll out and cut. Bake at 375° for 12-15 minutes. Makes 50-60 cookies.

Rolled Sugar Cookies (Key Recipe)

2¼ cups *sifted* whole wheat flour
1 tsp. baking powder
½ tsp. salt
¾ cup margarine or butter
1 cup raw or brown sugar
2 eggs, beaten
1 tsp. flavoring (½ lemon, ½ vanilla)

Sift together, twice, the flour, baking powder and salt. Cream butter, sugar, eggs and flavoring. Add dry ingredients. This will make a soft dough. Chill at least 1 hour. Roll out ⅛" thick. Cut into desired shapes. Place on ungreased baking sheet. Bake 6-8 minutes at 375°-400°.

Cinnamon Pecan Bars

Use key recipe. Mix into dough 1 cup finely chopped nuts. Roll out ½" thick and cut into oblongs 1½" x 3". Sprinkle with mixture of 2 tbsp. brown sugar and 2 tsp. cinnamon. Press ½ pecan nut into each bar. Bake 6-8 minutes at 375°-400°.

Filled Sugar Cookies

Use key recipe. Cut out 2" round cookies. Put 1 tsp. raisin filling on ½ of the cookies and cover with the other half. Press edges firmly with fork. Bake 10-12 minutes at 375°-400°.

Filling:

1 cup ground or chopped raisins
¼ cup brown sugar
½ cup water
1 tbsp. whole wheat flour

Mix raisins and sugar well. Bring to boil and thicken with flour mixed with water. Bring to boil again, stirring constantly.

COOKIES

Peanut Butter Cookies

1½ cups *sifted* whole wheat flour
½ tsp. soda
1 tsp. baking powder
½ cup butter or margarine
1 cup raw or brown sugar
1 egg, well beaten
½ cup peanut butter
2 tbsp. cream

Sift together flour, soda and baking powder. Cream sugar and butter. Add beaten egg and peanut butter. Mix well. Add cream and sifted dry ingredients. Form in balls size of a marble and place on greased cookie sheet. Press both ways with fork. Bake about 8 minutes at 350°-375°.

Thumb Print Cookies

1 cup *sifted* whole wheat flour
½ tsp. baking powder
¼ tsp. salt
½ cup margarine or butter
⅓ cup brown sugar (packed)
1 egg, separated
½ tsp. vanilla
¾-1 cup nuts, finely chopped

Sift together, twice, the flour, baking powder and salt. Cream butter and sugar, egg yolk and vanilla. Add dry ingredients and mix well. Roll dough into balls (1 tsp. per ball). Beat egg white slightly with fork. Dip balls in egg white; roll in nuts. Place about 1" apart on ungreased baking sheet. Press thumb gently in center of each ball. Bake 10-12 minutes at 350°, or until set. If desired, fill thumbprints with colored icing for Christmas, Easter, etc.

Sour Cream Cookies

4 cups *sifted* whole wheat flour
1 tsp. baking powder
¼ tsp. salt
½ tsp. nutmeg
1 cup margarine or butter
2 cups brown sugar
2 eggs, beaten
1 tsp. vanilla
1 cup sour cream (1 cup canned milk plus 1 tbsp. vinegar or lemon juice)

Sift together, twice, the flour, baking powder, salt and nutmeg. Cream butter, sugar, beaten eggs and vanilla. Add dry ingredients alternately with sour cream. Working with one-half the dough at a time, roll out on floured board to ⅛" thickness. Cut in small rounds with cookie cutter. Place on greased cookie sheet and bake 8-10 minutes at 375°-400°.

Note: This recipe may be used for Raisin-Filled Cookies (filling below). For Mincemeat-Filled Cookies, add 1 cup chopped apples (cooked 5 minutes in 1 tbsp. water) to a 9-oz. pkg. mincemeat. Do not increase sugar.

COOKIES

Raisin-Filled Cookies

Filling:

1 lb. raisins, put through food chopper
¼ tsp. salt
2 tbsp. whole wheat flour
½ cup water
¼ cup raw or brown sugar

Combine all ingredients and cook 5 minutes. Cool. One cup chopped nuts may be added, if desired.

Dough:

6 cups *sifted* whole wheat flour
½ tsp. salt
2 tsp. baking powder
1 cup margarine or butter
2 cups raw or brown sugar
1 tsp. vanilla
2 eggs, beaten
¾ cup canned milk

Sift together, twice, the flour, salt and baking powder. Cream butter and sugar. Add vanilla and eggs and beat well. Add sifted dry ingredients alternately with milk. Dough will be soft. Use whole wheat flour on board and rolling pin and handle as little as possible Roll dough thin and cut with cookie cutter. Place spoonful of filling on one cookie and cover with another cookie. Press edges together. Bake on greased cookie sheet at 350°-375°.

Snickerdoodle Cookies

2½ cups *sifted* whole wheat flour
2 tsp. baking powder
1 tsp. cream of tartar
¼ tsp. salt
1 cup margarine or butter
1½ cups raw or brown sugar
1 tsp. vanilla
2 large eggs, beaten
¼ cup brown sugar
2 tsp. cinnamon

Sift together, twice, the flour, baking powder, cream of tartar and salt. Cream margarine and sugar. Add vanilla and beaten eggs. Add dry ingredients. Mix well and chill.
Mix brown sugar and cinnamon. Form dough into balls the size of a large marble and roll in sugar-cinnamon mixture. Place on greased cookie sheet 2" apart. Bake 8-10 minutes at 375°. Remove immediately from pan to prevent sticking. Makes about 4 dozen cookies.

Crisp Gingersnaps

3½ cups *unsifted* whole wheat flour
1 tsp. cream of tartar
2 tsp. baking powder
½ tsp. soda
1 tsp. ginger
½ tsp. cloves
3 tsp. cinnamon
¾ cup oil
2 cups raw or brown sugar
½ cup molasses
2 eggs, beaten

Sift together flour, cream of tartar, baking powder, soda and spices. Cream oil, sugar and eggs. Add molasses and dry ingredients. Mix well and chill. Form dough into balls the size of a large marble. Place on greased cookie sheet 2" apart. Bake 11 minutes at 350°. Remove immediately from pan to prevent sticking.

Variation: Leave cream of tartar out and a softer cookie results. Makes 6 dozen cookies.

COOKIES

Crunchy Cookies

1¼ cups *sifted* whole wheat flour
2 tsp. baking powder
½ tsp. salt
½ cup margarine or butter
2 cups brown sugar
1 tsp. almond extract
2 eggs, beaten
2½ cups quick-cooking oatmeal
1 cup coconut
½ cup chopped nuts
3 cups cornflakes

Sift together, twice, the flour, baking powder and salt. Cream butter and sugar. Add almond extract and eggs. Blend in dry ingredients. Add oatmeal, nuts, coconut and corn flakes. Shape into 1" balls and press flat with fork. Bake 10-12 minutes at 375°.

Soft Molasses Ginger Cookies

3 cups *sifted* whole wheat flour
¾ tsp. salt
2 tsp. baking powder
1 tsp. ginger
1 tsp. cinnamon
1 cup butter or margarine
1 cup raw or brown sugar
2 eggs
½ cup molasses
½ cup evaporated milk

Sift together, twice, the flour, salt, baking powder and spices. Cream together butter and sugar. Beat in eggs and molasses. Add dry ingredients alternately with milk. Add coconut. Drop on greased cookie sheet and bake 8-10 minutes at 350°-375°.

Oatmeal Cookies

1 cup *sifted* whole wheat flour
½ tsp. salt
½ tsp. soda
¾ cup butter or margarine
1½ cup brown or raw sugar
1 egg
¼ cup water
1 tsp. vanilla
3 cups oatmeal

Sift together, twice, the flour, salt and soda. Cream butter, sugar and egg. Add water and vanilla with sifted dry ingredients and oatmeal. Drop by teaspoons onto greased cookie sheets. Bake 12-15 minutes at 350°. Do not overbake. For variety add chopped raisins or currants or nuts. Makes about 5 dozen.

Raisin Drop Cookies

3 cups *sifted* whole wheat flour
½ tsp. salt
2 tsp. baking powder
1½ cups raisins
¾ cup water
½ tsp. soda
½ cup butter or margarine
1½ cups raw or brown sugar
2 eggs, beaten

Sift together, twice, the flour, salt and baking powder. Boil raisins in water 2 minutes. Add soda and set aside to cool. Cream butter and sugar and add beaten eggs. Add dry ingredients alternately with raisins mixture. Bake 12-15 minutes at 350°-375°.

Variation: Add ½ cup candied fruit mix and boil with raisins and water.

COOKIES

Carrot Cookies (Cooked Carrots)

2 cups *sifted* whole wheat flour
2 tsp. baking powder
½ tsp. salt
¾ cup raw or brown sugar
¾ cup margarine or butter
1 tsp. vanilla
2 eggs, beaten
1 cup cooked mashed carrots (about 4)
½ cup shredded coconut and/or
1 cup chopped nuts

Sift together, twice, the flour, baking powder and salt. Cream sugar and butter. Add vanilla and eggs. Beat well. Add mashed carrots. Add dry ingredients and beat. Add coconut or nuts. Drop with a teaspoon onto greased cookie sheet. Bake 12-15 minutes at 350°-375°.

Cool and frost with following icing, if desired:

1¾-2 cups sifted powdered sugar
½ tsp. orange rind
2-3 tbsp. orange juice

Carrot Cookies (Raw Carrots)

2 cups *sifted* whole wheat flour
2 tsp. baking powder
¼ tsp. salt
1 cup raw or brown sugar
1 cup butter or margarine
1 tsp. vanilla
1 egg
1 cup finely grated raw carrot
2 tsp. grated orange rind

Sift together, twice, the flour, baking powder and salt. Cream together sugar and margarine. Add vanilla and egg and beat well. Stir in grated carrot and orange rind. Blend in dry ingredients. Drop by teaspoons on greased cookie sheet and bake 10-15 minutes at 375°.

Applesauce Cookies

2 cups *sifted* whole wheat flour
1 tsp. baking powder
½ tsp. salt
½ tsp. soda
¼ tsp. cloves
1 tsp. cinnamon
1 cup raw or brown sugar
½ cup butter or margarine
1 cup thick unsweetened applesauce
1 cup raisins
1 cup nuts, optional

Sift together, twice, the flour, baking powder, salt, soda and spices. Cream sugar and butter. Add egg and beat well. Add dry ingredients alternately with applesauce. Add raisins. If applesauce is quite thin, use 2½ cups flour. Drop by teaspoon on greased cookie sheet and bake 12-15 minutes at 350°-375°. Makes 3½-4 dozen cookies.

Whole Wheat Macaroons

1½ cups *sifted* whole wheat flour
½ tsp. salt
2 tsp. baking powder
¾ cup butter or margarine
1¼ cups raw or brown sugar
1 tsp. vanilla
2 eggs, beaten
3-4 tbsp. milk
2 cups oatmeal
1-1½ cups coconut

Sift together, twice, the flour, salt and baking powder. Cream butter and sugar. Add vanilla and eggs and beat well. Add dry ingredients alternately with milk. Stir in oatmeal and coconut. Drop by teaspoons on greased cookie sheet and bake 10-12 minutes at 350°-375°, or until delicately brown. Makes about 4 dozen cookies.

Variation: 1 cup chocolate chips or 1 cup nuts or 1 cup raisins instead of coconut. When substituting any of these, use 1¾ cups flour instead of 1½ cups.

Butterscotch Cookies

2½ cups *sifted* whole wheat flour
1 tsp. soda
½ tsp. baking powder
½ tsp. salt
½ cup butter or margarine
1½ cups raw or brown sugar
2 eggs, beaten
1 tsp. vanilla
1 cup sour cream (canned milk soured with 1 tbsp. vinegar or lemon juice)
⅔ cup nuts

Sift dry ingredients together twice. Cream butter, sugar, vanilla and eggs. Add dry ingredients with sour cream. Use ½ cup more flour if dough seems too thin. Drop rounded teaspoonsful on greased cookie sheet. Bake 10 minutes at 350°-375°. If desired, frost with Brown Butter Icing.

Brown-Butter Icing

½ cup butter (no substitute)
2 cups sifted powdered sugar
2-3 tbsp. boiling water
½ tsp. vanilla

Melt butter in small saucepan. Continue to cook until butter stops bubbling and is nut brown. Pour over sugar and beat, adding enough water to make right spreading consistency. Add vanilla.

Drop Sugar Cookies

1 cup *sifted* whole wheat flour
¼ cup wheat germ
½ cup powdered milk
2 tsp. baking powder
½ cup margarine or butter
¾ cup raw or brown sugar
1 tsp. vanilla
2 eggs, beaten
3 tbsp. canned milk

Sift together, twice, dry ingredients. Cream together butter, sugar, vanilla and eggs. Add dry ingredients to creamed mixture with canned milk. Blend well. Drop on cookie sheet. Bake 8-10 minutes at 350°. If desired, sprinkle with sugar.

Pineapple Cookies

4 cups *sifted* whole wheat flour
½ tsp. salt
3 tsp. baking powder
1 cup butter or margarine
1½ cups raw or brown sugar
1 tsp. vanilla
2 eggs
1 cup crushed pineapple, drained
1 cup chopped nuts

Sift together, twice, the flour, salt and baking powder. Cream butter and sugar. Add vanilla, then eggs and beat well. Add sifted dry ingredients alternately with crushed pineapple. Add nuts. Drop on greased cookie sheet and bake 10-12 minutes at 350°-375°.

COOKIES

Banana-Oatmeal Cookies

1¾ cups *sifted* whole wheat flour
2 tsp. baking powder
½ tsp. salt
¼ tsp. nutmeg
¾ cup margarine or butter
1 cup brown or raw sugar
1 tsp. vanilla
1 egg, well beaten
1 cup crushed bananas (2-3)
1½ cups quick-cooking oatmeal
½-1 cup chopped nuts (optional)

Sift together, twice, the flour, baking powder, salt and nutmeg. Cream butter and sugar. Add vanilla and beaten egg. Add mashed bananas and oatmeal, then dry ingredients. Add nuts. Drop with teaspoon onto greased cookie sheet. Bake 12-15 minutes at 375°. Makes about 4 dozen.

Coconut Drop Cookies

2 cups *sifted* whole wheat flour
2½ tsp. baking powder
½ tsp. salt
½ cup margarine or butter
2 cups raw or brown sugar
2 eggs, well beaten
1 tsp. vanilla
1 cup shredded coconut
1 cup cornflakes

Sift flour, baking powder and salt together twice. Cream butter and sugar until light. Add eggs and vanilla. Blend in dry ingredients. Add coconut and cornflakes. Drop with teaspoon onto greased cookie sheet. Bake 12-15 minutes at 350°.

Pineapple Squares

Base:

2 cups *sifted* whole wheat flour
1 cup margarine or butter
2 tbsp. raw or brown sugar
¼ tsp. salt

Blend until crumbly. Bake about 10 minutes in 9" x 12" pan at 375°, or until light brown.

Filling:

1 can (1 lb. 4 oz.) crushed
   pineapple, undrained
½ cup brown or raw sugar
2 tbsp. cornstarch
2 egg yolks, beaten
4-oz. bottle maraschino cherries,
   drained and cut up
¼ cup cold water

Cook pineapple, sugar, cornstarch, water and egg yolks until thick. Cool. Add cherries. Spread over base.

Topping:

2 egg whites, stiffly beaten
¼ cup brown sugar
⅛ tsp. salt
¼ tsp. almond flavoring

Spread over filling and sprinkle with coconut. Put under broiler until golden brown. Cool and cut into squares.

COOKIES

Raw Apple Cookies

4 cups *sifted* whole wheat flour
4 tsp. baking powder
3 tsp. cinnamon
1 tsp. allspice
1 cup margarine or butter
2 cups raw or brown sugar
1 tsp. vanilla
4 eggs
3 cups raw apple, grated or put through food chopper
1 cup chopped raisins
1 cup chopped walnuts

Sift together, twice, the flour, baking powder and spices. Cream margarine and sugar. Add vanilla and eggs, one at a time, mixing with medium speed for 1 minute. Add dry ingredients alternately with apples. Add raisins and nuts. Drop with teaspoon onto well-greased cookie sheet and bake 12-15 minutes at 350°. Makes 7-8 dozen medium-size cookies.

Note: This recipe can also be used for loaf or layer cake. If a food grinder is being used for the apples, put the raisins through at the same time.

Caramel Nut Squares

½ cup margarine or butter
1 cup *sifted* whole wheat flour
1 beaten egg
¼ tsp. salt, sifted with flour

Cut butter into flour as in making pastry. Add egg and mix well. Spread in 8" x 12" pan and bake 15 minutes at 350°. Remove and spread immediately with topping:

Topping:

2 eggs, beaten
1½ cups brown sugar
2 tbsp. whole wheat flour
½ tsp. baking powder
1 tsp. vanilla
¾ cup chopped nuts
½ cup shredded coconut

Blend eggs and brown sugar together. Sift flour and baking powder together and blend with egg mixture.
Add vanilla, nuts and coconut.

Spread on baked crust and return to 350° oven for 25-30 minutes.

Cool and cut into squares.

COOKIES

Carob Brownies

¾ cup *sifted* whole wheat flour
1 tsp. baking powder
½ tsp. salt
½ cup margarine or butter
½ cup raw or brown sugar
2 eggs, beaten
⅓ cup carob powder, plus ⅓ cup water
  (or 2 squares baking chocolate,
  melted with butter)
½ cup chopped walnuts

Sift dry ingredients together twice. Cream sugar and eggs and margarine. Add carob. Stir in dry ingredients. Bake in 8" square pan 25-30 minutes at 350°.

Prize-Winning Brownies

1 cup *sifted* whole wheat flour
¼ tsp. salt
1 tsp. baking powder
1 cup raw or brown sugar
2 tbsp. butter
1 tsp. vanilla
1 egg
*2 squares chocolate, melted
½ cup canned milk
1 cup nuts

*6 tbsp. carob powder, plus 4 tbsp. liquid
  (water or milk) equals 2 squares chocolate.

Cream together sugar, butter and vanilla. Add egg and beat well until light and fluffy. Add melted chocolate, sifted dry ingredients and canned milk. Mix well and stir in nuts. Pour into buttered 9" x 9" pan and bake 30-35 minutes at 350.°

Date-Nut Bars

1 cup sifted whole wheat flour
1 tsp. baking powder
¼ tsp. salt
3 eggs, separated
1 cup raw or brown sugar
1 cup chopped nuts
2 cups chopped dates

Sift dry ingredients together twice and combine with dates and nuts. Beat egg yolks until yellow and thick. Add sugar while beating constantly. Add flour-date mixture. Blend in stiffly beaten egg whites. Spread in greased 9" square pan and bake 30 minutes at 325°-350°. While warm cut into finger-length strips and sprinkle with powdered sugar, if desired.

Butterscotch Picnic Bars

2½ cups *sifted* whole wheat flour
3 tsp. baking powder
½ tsp. salt
⅔ cup butter or margarine or
  ¾ cup oil
2¼ cups brown or raw sugar, packed
4 eggs, well beaten
¾ cup quick-cooking oatmeal
6-oz. pkg. (1 cup) butterscotch
  morsels
¾ cup chopped nuts
1 cup raisins, optional

Sift together, twice, the flour, baking powder and salt. Melt butter in saucepan. Stir in sugar. Cool. Add beaten eggs. Beat until smooth. Add dry ingredients and blend. Add butterscotch morsels and nuts. Mix well. Spread evenly in 15" x 10" x 1" pan and bake 25 minutes at 350°. Cool and cut into 50 bars.

Variation: Substitute chocolate chips, if desired.

COOKIES

Raisin-Nut Squares (Bars)

1¼ cups *sifted* whole wheat flour
2 tsp. baking powder
¼ tsp. salt
½ cup margarine or butter
1 cup brown sugar
1 large, or 2 small, eggs
2 tsp. vanilla
1 cup raisins, chopped
½ cup pecans or walnuts, chopped

Sift together, twice, the flour, baking powder and salt. Cream sugar and butter. Add vanilla. Beat until light and fluffy. Beat in egg. Stir in raisins and nuts with dry ingredients, mixing thoroughly. Pour into greased and floured 8" square pan. Spread dough evenly. Bake 25-30 minutes at 350°. Do not overbake. Remove from oven and let stand 10 minutes. Turn out and cut into squares or bars. Cool thoroughly before storing.

Spicy Drop Cookies

2 cups *sifted* whole wheat flour
1 tsp. cinnamon
¼ tsp. salt
2 tsp. baking powder
1 tsp. ginger
¼ tsp. cloves
¾ cup butter or margarine
1 cup brown sugar, packed
1 egg, slightly beaten
¼ cup molasses

Sift together, twice, the flour, spices, salt and baking powder. Cream butter and brown sugar until light. Beat in egg and molasses. Add sifted dry ingredients, and mix well. Chill. Form dough in balls the size of a walnut. Place on cookie sheets and press flat with fork or bottom of tumbler dipped in water. Bake about 12 minutes at 350°-375°. Makes about 4 dozen cookies.

Honey-Date Bars

1⅓ cups *sifted* whole wheat flour
1 tsp. baking powder
¼ tsp. salt
1 cup honey
3 eggs, well beaten
1 tsp. vanilla
1½ cups dates, pitted and cut up
1 cup chopped nuts

Sift together, twice, the flour, baking powder and salt. Mix honey, eggs and vanilla and beat well. Add sifted dry ingredients, dates and nuts. Spread in greased 13" x 9" pan. Bake 45 minutes at 350°. Cool in pan. Cut in 3" x 1" bars.

Filled Cupcakes

1½ cups *sifted* whole wheat flour
2 tsp. baking powder
⅛ tsp. salt
¼ cup butter or oil
⅔ cup raw or brown sugar
1 egg, beaten
⅔ cup milk

Sift together, twice, the flour, baking powder and salt. Cream butter and sugar. Add egg and beat. Add dry ingredients alternately with milk. Be sure to use paper baking cups. Put small amount of batter in paper cups in muffin tins. Add small amount of filling, then more batter and top with filling. Bake 20-25 minutes at 350°-375°. Makes 1 dozen cupcakes.

Filling:

½ cup raw or brown sugar
2 tsp. cinnamon
1 tbsp. whole wheat flour
½ cup chopped walnuts
2½ tbsp. butter, melted

COOKIES

Coconut-Nut Cookies, Yule Cookies, and Jumbo Raisin Cookies are guaranteed to be good travelers and "keepers." Wrap each layer in foil or transparent plastic wrap and pack in a metal or sturdy cardboard box lined with soft paper to prevent the cookies from shaking or shifting about.

Coconut-Nut Cookies

white of 2 eggs
⅔ cup raw or brown sugar
⅓ cup honey
1 cup shredded coconut
1 cup dates, finely cut
2 cups chopped walnuts or pecans
1-1½ cups shredded coconut, for
   rolling cookies

That's right—no flour is used in this recipe. We include the recipe because this chewy cookie helps to keep other cookies moist in shipping.

Beat egg whites stiff. Add sugar to make a meringue. Add honey, chopped nuts, dates and 1 cup coconut. Mix well. Drop by teaspoon onto coconut and roll until thoroughly coated. Place on greased cookie sheet and bake 15-20 minutes at 325°-350° until slightly browned. Do not remove from cookie sheet until completely cooled or the cookie will collapse.

Yule Cookies

2½-2¾ cups *sifted* whole wheat flour
½ tsp. salt
1 tsp. baking powder
1 cup margarine or butter
2 cups brown or raw sugar
½ cup honey
3 large eggs, or 4 small
¼ cup orange juice
1 tbsp. grated orange rind
3 tbsp. lemon juice
1 tsp. grated lemon rind
3 tbsp. lemon juice
1 apple, coarsely grated
2 cups quick-cooking oatmeal
1 cup raisins
1 lb. fruit cake mix
1½ cups coarsely chopped nuts

Sift together, twice, the flour, salt and baking powder. Cream sugar and butter. Add honey and eggs and beat until light. Add all the fruits and fruit juices, beating after each addition. Add dry ingredients and blend. Add oatmeal and nuts. Blend and chill. Drop on greased cookie sheet. Flatten lightly with fork. Bake 12-15 minutes at 350°. Store in tightly-covered container.

COOKIES

Jumbo Raisin Cookies

4 cups *sifted* whole wheat flour
2 tsp. baking powder
½ tsp. soda
1 tsp. salt
1 tsp. cinnamon
¼ tsp. nutmeg
2 cups raisins
1 cup water
1 cup oil
2 cups raw or brown sugar
1 tsp. vanilla
3 eggs, beaten
1 cup chopped nuts

Sift together, twice, the flour, baking powder, soda, salt, and spices and sugar. Boil raisins in water 5 minutes. Cool. Drain raisins in a colander placed in bowl. Save 4 or 5 tbsp. of the juice and add to dry ingredients, together with oil, vanilla, beaten eggs and nuts. Mix thoroughly. Drop by large spoonsful onto greased baking sheet. Don't overcrowd. Bake 10 minutes at 375°. Makes about 4 dozen large cookies.

Variations:

Use ½ cup of juice plus 2 cups quick-cooking oatmeal for oatmeal cookies.

Use all of juice and enough water to make 1 cup liquid. Mix in the same way. Makes a good raisin cake. Bake in 9" x 13" dripper pan or a 13-¾" x 17-¾" sheet cake pan. Bake 40-45 minutes at 350°.

CAKES

General Suggestions

Flour for cakes and cookies should always be sifted once before measuring, then twice with other dry ingredients.

Whole wheat flour can be substituted for white flour in any good cake recipe. If whole wheat *pastry* flour is available, simply substitute it for white flour without changing the amount. If regular whole wheat flour is used, substitute 7/8 cup of *sifted* whole wheat flour for 1 cup of *sifted* white flour, and add 1 teaspoon more of baking powder and 1 more egg to the recipe. Separate eggs and fold in stiffly beaten egg whites last.

If you have an electric mixer, use it to save time and labor. Generally speaking, we find the following procedure very satisfactory for mixing cake batter with an electric mixer.

Cream butter at low speed, add sugar, beat at higher speed until creamy. Add extract at this point—it adheres to the fat and produces a better flavor. Turn to high speed and add eggs or egg yolks one at a time, beating thoroughly. Turn to low speed and add sifted dry ingredients alternately with liquid. Mix only until ingredients are blended, scraping batter from sides of bowl with rubber spatula as bowl revolves. Overbeating will cause toughness in a cake. Remember, even at low speed the mixer is twice as powerful as hand beating. To play safe, turn off mixer a little too soon and finish the last bit of mixing by hand.

Using water instead of milk will produce a lighter cake. If the extra nutritional value of milk is desired, use noninstant powdered milk, by sifting 1/3 to 1/2 cup of noninstant powdered milk with other dry ingredients, and use water in place of the fluid milk called for. For a lighter cake see also Dough Conditioner under Know Your Ingredients.

Do not overbake any cake.

Cake fillings and sauces require considerably less sugar and contain larger amounts of milk, eggs and nuts than do most icings; therefore, they are nutritionally superior to icings. In making icing, add some noninstant powdered milk to the powdered sugar. It will add nutrition without sacrificing flavor. With 1½-2 cups of powdered sugar, ½ to ¾ cup of noninstant powdered milk may be used. Alternatively, powdered whey can also be used. (See Whey, under Know Your Ingredients.)

Perfect Plain Whole Wheat Cake

(*Serve with your favorite topping or sauce.*)

½ cup margarine
1½ cups raw or brown sugar
2 tsp. vanilla
3 eggs, separated
1 cup water
2 cups *sifted* whole wheat flour
3 tsp. baking powder
½ tsp. salt
½ cup powdered milk

Use electric mixer if possible. Cream margarine, sugar, and vanilla. Add egg yolks, one at a time, beating well after each addition. Sift dry ingredients together twice and add alternately with water. Fold in beaten egg whites last.

Bake in well-greased 8" x 12" pan 30-35 minutes at 350°.

CAKES

Orange-Whipped Cream Sauce

¼ cup honey
¾ cup orange juice
½ tsp. grated orange rind
2 egg yolks, beaten
1 cup whipping cream

Combine honey, orange juice, orange rind and beaten egg yolks in double boiler and cook until thick. Chill thoroughly and blend in whipped cream just before serving.

Pineapple Filling

no. 2½ can crushed pineapple, drained
2 tbsp. cornstarch
¼ cup honey
4 tbsp. orange juice

Combine pineapple, cornstarch and honey. Cook 10 minutes. Add orange juice. Chill before serving.

Spicy Peach Sauce

1 qt. canned peaches, sliced
¼ cup brown sugar
¼ cup water
¼ tsp. salt
2 tbsp. cornstarch
1 tbsp. butter
¼ tsp. nutmeg

Drain juice from peaches and set fruit aside. Rinse jar with ¼ cup water. Bring fruit juice and water to boil. Combine sugar, salt and cornstarch and stir into boiling juice. Cook 5 minutes. Remove from heat and add butter and nutmeg. Stir in drained, sliced peaches.

Whipped Banana Topping

1 large egg white, stiffly beaten
2 tbsp. honey
1 banana, mashed well

Whip egg white until stiff. Add honey gradually, beating well after each addition. Add mashed banana and mix well. Serve immediately.

Variation: This topping is delicious made with 1 cup of other mashed fruit or berries, well drained.

Thrifty Pineapple Topping or Filling

1 lb. 4 oz. can crushed pineapple
½ cup honey
⅞ cup water
3 tsp. (1 envelope) unflavored gelatin

Combine all ingredients in double boiler. Stir well and cook for 10 minutes. Chill thoroughly before using. Other cooked fruit may be substituted for pineapple.

CAKES

Crunchy Topping

1 cup regular rolled oats
1 cup rolled wheat flakes
1 cup All-Bran
1 cup Grapenuts (see Wheatnuts)
1 cup sesame seeds
1 cup coconut chips or flakes
1 cup sunflower seeds
1 cup pumpkin seeds (optional)
2/3 cup butter (no substitute)
1 cup raw or brown sugar

Mix all together well. Place on large cookie sheet. Toast 15 minutes in 325°-350° oven. Use on desserts and ice cream. Delicious sprinkled on top of whipped cream for a cake topping.

Spice Cake

2 cups *sifted* whole wheat flour
1/2 tsp. soda
2 tsp. baking powder
3/4 tsp. salt
1/2 tsp. nutmeg
1 tsp. cinnamon
1/4 tsp. cloves
1/2 cup butter or margarine
1 cup raw or brown sugar
2 eggs
1 cup buttermilk or sour milk

Sift dry ingredients together twice. Cream butter and sugar. Beat in eggs one at a time. Add buttermilk alternately with sifted dry ingredients. Bake in layer pans or in 8" x 12" pan 30 minutes at 350°-375°. Cup cakes may be made from this recipe. One cup raisins and 1/2 cup chopped nuts may be added. Add these to the dry ingredients for easier mixing. Frost with your choice of icings.

Divinity Frosting

1 cup raw or brown sugar
⅓ cup water
1 tbsp. corn syrup
⅛ tsp. salt
2 egg whites, beaten

Cook sugar, water, syrup and salt until it spins a thread. Pour slowly over well-beaten egg whites. When thick and cool, spread on cake.

Broiled Coconut Icing

4 tbsp. butter
½ cup brown or raw sugar
2 tbsp. milk
1 cup shredded coconut

Combine butter, brown sugar and milk in saucepan and bring to a boil. Remove from heat and add coconut. Pour over warm cake spreading evenly. Place cake in middle of oven. Turn oven control to broil position and broil slowly until a golden brown, 2-3 minutes.

Coconut Cake

2 cups *sifted* whole wheat flour
½ tsp. salt
2 tsp. baking powder
½ tsp. soda
¾ cup canned milk
¼ cup water (add 1 tbsp. lemon juice to milk and water to sour milk)
½ cup butter or margarine
1 cup raw or brown sugar
2 eggs, separated
1 tsp. vanilla

Combine water and milk and lemon juice. Set aside to sour. Sift the dry ingredients together twice. Cream butter and sugar. Add vanilla and egg yolks and beat well. Add sifted dry ingredients to creamed mixture alternately with sour milk. Fold in beaten egg whites. Bake in layers 20 minutes at 350°-375°. Frost with Maple Seafoam Frosting.

CAKES

Never-Fail Sheet Cake with Topping

3 cups *sifted* whole wheat flour
4½ tsp. baking powder
¾ tsp. salt
⅔ cup butter or margarine
1½ cups raw or brown sugar
1 tsp. vanilla
3 eggs
1½ cups milk

Sift the dry ingredients together twice. Cream butter and sugar and add vanilla. Add eggs and beat for 2 minutes. Add dry ingredients alternately with milk. Blend well. Pour into greased sheet pan 17¾" x 11¾". Sprinkle with topping.

Topping:
½ cup raw or brown sugar
2 tbsp. butter (unmelted)
2 tbsp. whole wheat flour
½ cup nuts and/or coconut

Bake 25-30 minutes at 350°-375°. This cake dough may also be used for layer cake or cup cakes.

Maple Seafoam Frosting

1 cup dark Karo
1 egg white, beaten
2 drops maple flavoring
½ cup shredded coconut

Boil syrup 2 minutes. Beat egg white. Pour hot syrup slowly over egg white, beating constantly. Add flavoring and continue beating until cool. Spread on cake and sprinkle with shredded coconut. Set under broiler until coconut is golden brown.

Soft Gingerbread

3 cups *sifted* whole wheat flour
1 tsp. soda
1 tsp. ginger
1 tbsp. cinnamon
1 tsp. cloves
½ tsp. salt
1 cup raw or brown sugar
1 cup oil
3 eggs, well beaten
1 cup sour milk
1 cup molasses (if using blackstrap, cut to ½ cup)

Sift dry ingredients together twice. Combine in mixing bowl the sugar, oil, eggs, sour milk and molasses. Beat in dry ingredients and bake in greased and floured 8" x 12" pan 35-45 minutes at 350°-375°, or until firm when touched with fingertip.

CAKES

Prize Sponge Cake

6 large eggs, separated
1½ cups raw or brown sugar
½ cup water
½ tsp. vanilla
½ tsp. lemon juice or lemon extract
¼ tsp. almond extract
1½ cups *sifted* whole wheat flour
¼ tsp. salt
1 tsp. cream of tartar

Beat with electric mixer the yolks, water, sugar, flavorings for 5-7 minutes, using small mixer bowl, then transfer to a larger bowl. Mixture must be *very* thick and creamy. Sift flour and salt together twice. Add to above mixture gradually, continuing to beat with mixer on low speed. Beat egg whites and cream of tartar together until stiff. Do not underbeat and do not allow whites to stand, but fold immediately into first mixture. Bake in ungreased tube pan 60-70 minutes, or until top springs back when lightly touched, at 325° 350°. Invert pan and cool thoroughly before removing. Serves 16. Delicious served with whipped cream and fresh fruit or Crunchy Topping.

Chiffon Cake

1 cup *sifted* whole wheat flour
¾ cup raw or brown sugar
1½ tsp. baking powder
¼ tsp. salt
¼ cup oil
2 egg yolks, unbeaten
⅜ cup (¼ cup plus 2 tbsp.) cold water
1 tsp. grated lemon rind
1 tsp. vanilla
½ cup egg whites (4)
¼ tsp. cream of tartar

Sift dry ingredients together twice into small mixer bowl. Make a well and add oil, egg yolks, water and flavorings. Beat until *very* smooth.

In a large mixer bowl, beat egg whites and cream of tartar into very stiff peaks. Do not underbeat. Pour egg yolk mixture slowly over beaten egg whites, folding gently with rubber scraper until barely blended. Don't stir. Pour immediately into ungreased 8" or 9" square pan. Bake 30-35 minutes at 350°-375° or until top springs back when lightly touched. Turn pan upside down, resting edges on 2 other pans. Let hang, free of table, until cold. Loosen sides with spatula; turn pan over and hit edges sharply on table to loosen. This can also be baked in tube pan, by doubling recipe and baking time.

Date Cake

1 cup chopped dates
1 cup boiling water
1 tsp. soda
1½ cups *sifted* whole wheat flour
½ tsp. salt
1 egg, beaten
1 cup raw or brown sugar
1 tsp. vanilla
⅔ cup oil or melted butter
½ cup nuts

Pour boiling water over dates, add soda and set aside to cool. Sift flour and salt together twice. In mixing bowl, beat egg and add sugar, vanilla and oil. Add dry ingredients alternately with date-water mixture. Bake in 8" x 12" pan 35-45 minutes at 350°-375°. Remove from oven and quickly cover with topping. Return to oven 10 minutes more.

Topping:

½ cup brown sugar
¼ cup *unsifted* whole wheat flour
¼ cup melted butter
2 tbsp. water
¾ cup nuts

Combine all ingredients and cover top of Date Cake.

Prune Cake

2 cups *sifted* whole wheat flour
2 tsp. baking powder
½ tsp. salt
½ cup butter or margarine
1 cup raw or brown sugar
2 eggs
½ cup milk
1 cup stewed prunes (chopped fine)
⅓ cup nuts
1 tsp. soda
2 tbsp. water

Sift together flour, baking powder and salt. Cream butter and sugar. Beat in eggs. Add milk alternately with dry ingredients. Add prunes and nuts. Dissolve soda in water and add last. Beat well. Bake in layer pans 30 minutes at 350°-375°. Frost with Divinity Icing.

Note: Double recipe and bake in 11¾" x 17¾" sheet cake pan.

Carob Frosting

2 tbsp. butter
⅔ cup noninstant powdered milk
⅓ cup carob powder
¼ cup honey
4 tbsp. cream
1 tsp. vanilla

Cream butter with powdered milk. Add carob powder. Mix well. Add honey, cream and vanilla. Beat until smooth and spread on cool cake. (1 tbsp. hot water may be added if necessary for easier spreading.)

Chocolate Sour Cream Cake

2 cups *sifted* whole wheat flour
1 tsp. baking powder
½ tsp. salt
¼ cup butter or margarine
1 cup raw or brown sugar
2 eggs, separated
1 cup sour cream (canned milk may be soured with 1 tbsp. vinegar)
2 squares melted chocolate
1 tsp. vanilla
1 tsp. soda
3 tbsp. boiling water

Sift together, twice, the flour, baking powder and salt. Cream butter, sugar and egg yolks. Add sour cream alternately with sifted dry ingredients. Beat in melted chocolate and vanilla. Add soda dissolved in boiling water and beat. Fold in beaten egg whites. Pour into two layer cake pans and bake 20 minutes at 350°-375°. This cake may also be baked in 8" x 12" pan 35-45 minutes.

Note: Chocolate may be replaced with 5-6 tbsp. of Carob Powder, plus 4 tbsp. liquid (milk or water). Use ½ tsp. soda and 2 tsp. baking powder.

Pineapple Upside-Down Cake

Topping:

2 tbsp. butter
½ cup brown sugar
9 slices pineapple
9 maraschino cherries

Batter:

1 cup *sifted* whole wheat flour
¼ tsp. salt
1½ tsp. baking powder
2 eggs
½ cup raw or brown sugar
1 tsp. vanilla
½ cup hot milk
2 tbsp. butter

Melt 2 tbsp. butter in 9" square pan and add brown sugar. Arrange pineapple slices and cherries over this. Sift together, twice, the flour, salt and baking powder. For batter, beat eggs well. Add sugar gradually, then vanilla. Add sifted dry ingredients alternately with mixture of hot milk and butter. Pour over pineapple. Bake 40-45 minutes at 350°-375°. Remove from oven and let stand 10 minutes. Invert on serving plate. Serve with whipped cream.

Banana-Nut Loaf Cake

2 cups *sifted* whole wheat flour
¼ tsp. salt
2 large bananas
¼ cup butter
1½ cups raw or brown sugar
2 eggs, separated
1 tsp. soda
2 tbsp. sour milk
1 cup chopped walnuts

Sift together, twice, the flour and salt. Mash and cream bananas. Add butter, sugar and egg yolks. Cream thoroughly. Dissolve soda in sour milk and add with flour. Stir in nuts. Fold in beaten egg whites. Bake in greased loaf pan 45 minutes at 350°-375°.

Economy (Eggless) Cake

2 cups raisins
1¼ cups water
⅓ cup oil or margarine
1 cup raw or brown sugar
½ tsp. nutmeg
2 tsp. cinnamon
½ tsp. cloves
2 cups *sifted* whole wheat flour
1 tsp. baking powder
1 tsp. salt
1 tsp. soda dissolved in
2 tsp. hot water

Cook raisins, water, oil, sugar and spices together for 3 minutes. Cool slightly. Add sifted dry ingredients and soda dissolved in water. Pour into greased and floured 8" square pan and bake 50 minutes at 325°-350°. This cake is delicious uniced.

Shortcake

(For strawberries or other fresh fruits.)

4 cups *sifted* whole wheat flour
6 tsp. baking powder
1 tsp. salt
1 cup raw or brown sugar
1 cup butter or margarine
1 cup milk
2 eggs, well beaten

Sift together, twice, the sifted whole wheat flour, baking powder and salt. Place in large mixing bowl. Add raw sugar and mix well with large spoon. Cut in butter with pastry blender. Add milk and eggs and mix until all flour is absorbed. Divide evenly in 2 layer pans. Bake 20 minutes at 375°-400°. Spread each cooled layer with sweetened whipped cream and crushed berries or other fruit. Place one on top of the other and cut for serving. If individual shortcakes are desired, roll or pat dough to ½" thickness on floured board. Cut with floured biscuit cutter. Bake on cookie sheet 20 minutes at 375°-400°. Spread the same as large cake. One half of this recipe is sufficient for a small family.

Boiled Raisin Cake

1½ cups raisins
2½ cups water
1 tsp. soda
3½ cups *sifted* whole wheat flour
½ tsp. salt
½ tsp. cinnamon
½ tsp. cloves
½ tsp. allspice
2 tsp. baking powder
½ cup butter or margarine
2 cups raw or brown sugar
2 eggs
1 tsp. vanilla
½ cup nuts

Boil for a few minutes raisins, water and soda. Set aside. Sift together, twice, the flour, salt, spices and baking powder. Cream butter, sugar, eggs and vanilla. Add hot raisin mixture to creamed mixture with dry ingredients and nuts. Beat. Mixture will be very thin. Pour into greased 9" x 13" pan. Bake 40-45 minutes at 350°.

This can be frosted as cake, or served as a pudding with your favorite sauce.

Ground-Raisin Cake

1½ cups raisins, ground
1 cup boiling water
1 tsp. soda
2 cups *sifted* whole wheat flour
½ tsp. baking powder
½ tsp. salt
1 tsp. nutmeg
½ cup butter or margarine
1 cup raw or brown sugar
1 tsp. lemon extract
2 eggs and 1 egg yolk (save
  1 egg white for icing)

Add soda to raisins, pour boiling water over. Set aside to cool. Sift together flour, baking powder, salt and nutmeg. Cream butter and sugar. Add flavoring. Add eggs and beat thoroughly. Add dry ingredients with raisin mixture. Bake in layer pans 20 minutes at 350°-375°. Ice with Seven-Minute Icing.

Seven-Minute Icing

¾ cup brown sugar
2½ tbsp. cold water
1 egg white
1 tsp. Karo syrup

Beat over boiling water until it won't drop from beater. Add vanilla or any preferred flavoring.

CAKES

Applesauce Cake

2 cups *sifted* whole wheat flour
2 tsp. baking powder
½ tsp. soda
½ tsp. salt
1 tsp. cinnamon
½ tsp. nutmeg
½ cup margarine or butter
1 cup brown or raw sugar
2 eggs, well beaten
1½ cups applesauce, heated
1 cup raisins
1 cup chopped nuts

Sift together, twice, the flour, salt, soda, baking powder and spices. Cream margarine, sugar and eggs. Beat well. Add applesauce alternately with dry ingredients. Stir in raisins and nuts. Bake in 9" square pan 30-35 minutes at 350°. If desired, pour topping for Oatmeal Cake over cake and place immediately under broiler until bubbly.

Fruit Cake

1 pkg. currants
1 lb. dates, pitted and cut
1 pkg. seeded raisins
1 lb. candied fruit mix
1 lb. chopped nuts
Grated rind and juice of 1 orange and 1 lemon
6 cups *sifted* whole wheat flour
1 tsp. baking powder
1 tsp. cloves
2 tsp. cinnamon
2 tsp. nutmeg
1 tsp. salt
3 cups brown sugar
1½ cups butter
6 eggs
½ cup molasses
½ cup sour milk
1 tsp. soda

Combine in very large container the currants, dates, raisins, fruit mix and nuts. Mix juice and grated rinds thoroughly. Sift together, twice, the flour, baking powder, salt and spices. Cream butter, sugar and eggs. Dissolve soda in sour milk and add with sifted dry ingredients and molasses. Combine batter and fruits thoroughly. Bake in 4 loaf tins lined with foil or waxed paper at 300°-325° about 2 hours or until toothpick inserted in loaf comes out clean. Cool. Wrap well in plastic and store or freeze.

CAKES

German Apple Streusel Cake

2 cups *sifted* whole wheat flour
2 tsp. baking powder
¾ tsp. salt
¾ cup milk
½ cup margarine or butter
1 cup raw or brown sugar
2 eggs
1 tsp. vanilla
4-5 apples

Peel and cut apples into thin slices. Sift together dry ingredients twice. Cream butter, sugar, eggs and vanilla. Add milk and sifted dry ingredients and beat until batter is smooth. Spread into 12" x 8" pan. Lay apple slices in rows on cake batter and cover with streusel mix.

Streusel Mix:

¼ lb. butter
¾ cup whole wheat flour
½ cup brown sugar
½ tsp. cinnamon

Cut butter into combined dry ingredients until texture is lumpy. Sprinkle over apples and bake until golden brown, about 45-50 minutes at 350°.

Dutch Hustle Cake

1½ cups *sifted* whole wheat flour
¼ tsp. salt
⅓ cup canned milk
⅓ cup boiling water
⅓ cup raw or brown sugar
½ tbsp. dry yeast, or 2 tsp. baking powder
2 eggs, beaten
2 tbsp. oil

Sift together, twice, the flour and salt. Combine milk, water and sugar. Mix in yeast and stir well. Let stand 5 minutes. Add beaten egg and oil, then sifted dry ingredients. Beat smooth. Spread dough evenly in greased 9" round cake pan and let stand while cooking the topping, as follows:

Topping:

2-3 apples, sliced
3 tbsp. brown sugar
3 tbsp. water

Cook 5 minutes. Cool. Arrange cooked apple slices on top of cake. Then sprinkle with mixture of 2 tbsp. brown sugar, ¼ tsp. cinnamon and ⅛ tsp. nutmeg.

Dot with 2 tbsp. margarine. Cover and let rise until cake is double in bulk when using yeast. Bake 30-35 minutes at 350°-375°.

Peach Crumbly Cake

1 can (1 lb.) sliced peaches
1¾ cups *sifted* whole wheat flour
1 cup raw or brown sugar
½ cup margarine or butter
2 tsp. baking powder
½ tsp. ginger
½ tsp. cinnamon
¼ tsp. mace or nutmeg
¼ tsp. salt
1 egg, beaten
¾ cup sour milk or buttermilk

Drain peaches. In mixing bowl, blend flour, sugar and margarine until crumbly. Set aside 1 cup "crumbs." Into remainder of "crumbs" mix baking powder, spices and salt. Add beaten egg and sour milk and blend. Spread ½ cup "crumb" mixture in bottom of greased 8" cake pan. Pour in batter carefully. Arrange sliced peaches on batter and sprinkle with remaining "crumbs." Bake 45-50 minutes at 350°.

Serve warm or cold, with or without whipped cream. Makes 6-8 servings.

New Zealand Apple Shortcake

2 cups *sifted* whole wheat flour
1 tsp. baking powder
⅓ cup cornstarch
¾ cup margarine or butter
½ cup raw or brown sugar
1 egg, beaten

Filling:

2 cups thick applesauce,
　or equivalent in fresh apples
½ tsp. cinnamon
½ cup brown sugar
1 tsp. lemon juice

Sift together, twice, the flour, baking powder and cornstarch. Cream butter and sugar. Add egg. Add dry ingredients. Divide dough into 2 portions. Roll each portion into an 8" square. Place one portion in an 8" cake pan. Mix filling ingredients well. Pour on top of dough in pan. Cover with other half of dough. Bake 30 minutes at 350°. Serve with custard sauce. (Vanilla pudding may be used for sauce.)

Swiss Spiced Carrot Cake

2¼ cups *sifted* whole wheat flour
4 tsp. baking powder
½ tsp. salt
1 tsp. cinnamon
½ tsp. mace or nutmeg
¾ cup margarine or butter
2 cups brown or raw sugar
1 tsp. vanilla
4 egg yolks, beaten
1½ cups grated raw carrots
⅔ cup chopped nuts
½ cup hot water

Sift together, twice, the flour, salt, baking powder and spices. Cream margarine and sugar. Add vanilla and beaten egg yolks. Stir in carrots and nuts. Add dry ingredients alternately with hot water. Spread batter in well-greased 12" x 8" pan lined with waxed paper. Bake 30-35 minutes at 350°-375° Cool and ice with Butterscotch Cream Icing.

CAKES

Pineapple Breakfast Cake

1½ cups *sifted* whole wheat flour
2 tsp. baking powder
½ tsp. salt
2 tbsp. noninstant powdered milk
¾ cup raw or brown sugar
¼ cup oil
2 eggs, beaten
½ cup water

Sift together, twice, the flour, baking powder, salt and powdered milk. Mix sugar, oil and eggs together, gradually stirring in water. Add dry ingredients. Blend. Do not overbeat. Spread batter in greased 9" square or round pan and sprinkle with pineapple topping (recipe below). Bake 25-30 minutes at 375°.

Pineapple Topping

3 tbsp. soft margarine or butter
3 tbsp. brown sugar
¾ cup drained crushed pineapple

Mix together thoroughly.

Oatmeal Cake with Broiled Topping

1½ cups boiling water
1 cup quick-cooking oatmeal
1½ cups *sifted* whole wheat flour
½ tsp. salt
2 tsp. baking powder
1 tsp. cinnamon
½ tsp. nutmeg
½ cup butter
1½ cups brown sugar
2 or 3 eggs
1 tsp. vanilla
¾ cup raisins (optional)

Pour boiling water over oatmeal and set aside. Sift together, twice, the flour, salt, baking powder and spices. Cream butter and sugar. Add eggs, one at a time, beating well after each addition. Stir in oatmeal mixture and sifted dry ingredients. Beat well. Add vanilla. Pour into greased and floured 13" x 9" x 2" pan. Bake 35 minutes at 350°. Remove from oven. Pour on topping immediately and place under broiler until topping is bubbly (2-3 minutes).

Broiled Topping

⅓ cup butter or margarine
½ cup brown sugar
½ cup milk
¾ cup coconut
⅓ cup chopped nuts

Melt butter in small saucepan. Add sugar and milk. Boil 1 minute. Stir in nuts and coconut.

Alternate Quick Topping

3 tbsp. melted butter or margarine
⅔ cup brown sugar
½ cup coconut
⅓ cup chopped nuts

Sprinkle over batter before baking.

Butterscotch Morsel-Date Cake

1½ cups boiling water
1 cup chopped dates
½ tsp. soda
1½ cups *sifted* whole wheat flour
½ tsp. salt
2 tsp. baking powder
½ cup butter or margarine
¾ cup brown sugar
2 eggs, beaten

Combine boiling water, dates and soda, and cool. Sift together, twice, the flour, salt and baking powder. Cream butter, sugar and eggs. Add dry ingredients alternately with date mixture. Blend well. Batter will be very thin. Pour into greased 9" x 13" pan and cover with topping made as follows:

Topping:

1 pkg. butterscotch morsels
½ cup chopped nuts
½ cup brown sugar

Mix together and sprinkle over batter. Bake about 40 minutes at 350°. Serve with whipped cream, if desired.

Raisin Cupcakes

2 cups seedless raisins
1 cup water
½ tsp. soda
1¾ cups *sifted* whole wheat flour
1 tsp. baking powder
¼ tsp. salt
½ cup margarine or butter
1 cup brown or raw sugar
2 eggs

Boil raisins, water and soda together 2 minutes. Sift together, twice, the flour, baking powder and salt. Cream butter and sugar. Add eggs. one at a time, beating well after each addition. Blend in raisin mixture alternately with sifted dry ingredients. Fill muffin tins ¾ full. Bake 30-35 minutes at 350°. Cool and frost with Butterscotch Cream Icing.

Butterscotch Cream Icing

¼ cup canned milk
3 tbsp. margarine or butter
½ cup firmly packed brown sugar
¼ tsp. vanilla
1¾ (about) cups sifted powdered sugar

Combine canned milk, margarine and brown sugar in small pan. Cook over medium heat, stirring constantly, until butter and sugar are melted. Remove from heat and add vanilla. Work in enough sifted powdered sugar to make of spreading consistency. Spread immediately on cake.

CAKES

Orange-Date Cake

2 cups *sifted* whole wheat flour
½ tsp. salt
3 tsp. baking powder
½ cup soft butter
1 cup raw or brown sugar
2 eggs, beaten
2 tbsp. grated orange rind
⅔ cup sour milk or buttermilk
1 cup chopped dates
½ cup chopped nuts
¼ cup whole wheat flour

Sift together, twice, the flour, salt and baking powder. Cream butter, sugar and eggs until fluffy. Add orange rind. Add sifted dry ingredients alternately with milk. Add chopped dates and nuts that have been floured with the ¼ cup flour. Turn into greased and floured 9" pan and bake 35-40 minutes at 350°.

While cake is baking, mix Orange Glaze. Allow to stand, stirring occasionally. When cake is baked and before removing from pan, pour over warm cake. Allow to cool in pan.

Orange Glaze:
juice of 1 orange
1 tbsp. grated orange rind
½ cup brown sugar

Orange Kiss-Me Cake

Rind of 1 orange (save juice for topping)
1 cup raisins
⅓ cup walnuts
2 cups *sifted* whole wheat flour
3 tsp. baking powder
½ tsp. salt
1 cup raw or brown sugar
½ cup margarine or butter
1 tsp. vanilla
2 eggs, well beaten
¾ cup milk

Grind orange rind, raisins and walnuts together. Sift together, twice, the flour, baking powder and salt. Cream sugar and butter. Add vanilla and well-beaten eggs. Add dry ingredients alternately with milk and beat until well blended. Stir in ground raisins, orange rind and walnuts. Bake in 12" x 8" pan, greased and floured 40-45 minutes at 350°.

Spread following mixture over warm cake:

¼ cup orange juice
¼ cup raw or brown sugar
1 tsp. cinnamon
¼ cup finely chopped nuts

DESSERTS

Canadian Apple Dumplings

1 cup *sifted* whole wheat flour
2 tsp. baking powder
½ tsp. salt
6 tbsp. butter or margarine
¼ cup milk
2 apples
½ cup brown sugar
½ tsp. cinnamon

Sift flour, baking powder and salt into a bowl. Cut in butter. Add milk and toss with a fork into a ball. Place on floured board and knead 10 times. Roll into oblong and cut into 4 squares.
Peel the apples and slice each apple half onto a square of dough. Sprinkle with mixture of brown sugar and cinnamon. Fold dough over apple and pinch sides of dough together. Place in buttered 8" pan or casserole and pour syrup on top (recipe below). Bake 40-45 minutes at 375°. Serve warm. Can be reheated next day.

Syrup:
½ cup brown sugar
⅛ tsp. cinnamon
2 tbsp. butter
1 cup water
⅛ tsp. nutmeg

Combine all ingredients. Boil 2 minutes. Makes syrup for 4 dumplings.

Apple Crunch Supreme

2 lbs. cooking apples (6-8)
¼ cup brown sugar
1 tsp. cinnamon
1 tsp. lemon juice
2 tbsp. water

Peel and slice apples into 9" x 13" pan. Sprinkle with mixture of sugar and cinnamon. Combine water and lemon juice and pour over apples.

Crunch Mixture:

1½ cups *sifted* whole wheat flour
1½ cups brown sugar
1 tsp. baking powder
1 tsp. salt
2 eggs
½ cup butter, melted

Mix all except butter with hands, sprinkle over apples. Pour melted butter over all. Bake 45 minutes at 350°. Serve with whipped cream, ice cream or Caramel Sauce.

Caramel Sauce

2 cups light brown sugar
1 cup Karo syrup (½ light, ½ dark)
½ cup margarine
1 tall can condensed milk (chilled)

Boil together sugar, syrup and margarine to soft ball stage. Cool 5 minutes. Beat in thoroughly chilled canned milk. Store in quart bottle in refrigerator. This sauce may also be used as topping for cake or ice cream.

Best-Ever Apple Pudding

2 cups *sifted* whole wheat flour
3 tsp. baking powder
1½ tsp. cinnamon
1 tsp. nutmeg
½ tsp. salt
2 cups raw or brown sugar
½ cup margarine or butter
2 eggs, beaten
5-6 (4 cups) grated, unpeeled apples
½ cup chopped nuts

Sift together flour, baking powder, spices and salt. Cream sugar and margarine. Add eggs and beat well. Add apples, sifted dry ingredients and nuts. Mix thoroughly and place in greased 9" x 13" pan. Bake 40-45 minutes at 350°. Serve with sauce and/or whipped cream, if desired.

Sauce:

1 cup raw or brown sugar
½ tsp. cinnamon
½ tsp. nutmeg
3 tbsp. cornstarch
2 cups boiling water
⅓ cup butter
2 tsp. vanilla

Combine sugar, spices and cornstarch and stir into boiling water. Bring to boil. Cook for 5 minutes, stirring constantly. Remove from heat and add butter and vanilla.

Fruit Crisp (Key Recipe)

(*Use this Key Recipe for topping for most fruits**: *apples, apricots, blueberries, boysenberries, cherries, rhubarb.*)

½ cup *sifted* whole wheat flour
½ cup quick-cooking oatmeal
¾ cup brown sugar
1 tsp. cinnamon
¼ cup butter

*Place in a buttered 1½-quart baking dish 3 cups of any of these fruits and add 2 tbsp. lemon juice. Fruit can be fresh or canned. Tart, fresh fruit will need 4-6 tbsp. additional sugar combined with the fruit before topping is added.

Combine all ingredients and cut in butter until mixture resembles coarse crumbs. Sprinkle over fruit mixture and bake 30-35 minutes at 350°. Serve warm or cold with whipped cream, ice cream or custard sauce. Serves six.

Fruit Cobbler (Key Recipe)

1½ cups *sifted* whole wheat flour
2 tbsp. raw or brown sugar
2 tsp. baking powder
½ tsp. salt
3 tbsp. butter or margarine
1 egg, well beaten, plus milk
    to make 1 cup liquid

Sift dry ingredients together 4 times. Blend in butter. Add liquid and blend, don't beat. Spread over sweetened fruit: apples, apricots, blueberries, boysenberries, cherries, rhubarb, peaches.

Bake at 350°-375° until fruit is tender. Serve with whipped cream, if desired.

DESSERTS

Date Pudding

⅔ cup whole wheat bread crumbs
⅔ cup raw or brown sugar
½ cup milk
1 tsp. baking powder
2 eggs, beaten
3 tbsp. melted butter
1 cup chopped dates
1 cup chopped nuts
½ tsp. salt

Combine all ingredients and place in greased 8" square pan. Bake in pan of water 40-50 minutes at 350°-375°. Serve whipped cream.

Mystery Pudding

1 cup *sifted* whole wheat flour
½ tsp. salt
½ tsp. soda
2 tsp. baking powder
½ cup brown sugar
½ cup syrup from fruit cocktail
2 eggs, beaten
1½ cups (no. 2½ can) fruit cocktail, drained
½ cup chopped nuts
¼ cup brown sugar

Sift together, twice, the flour, salt, soda and baking powder. Add ½ cup brown sugar, fruit cocktail syrup and eggs. Blend well. Stir in drained fruit cocktail and nuts. Mix well and turn into a greased 8" or 9" square baking pan. Sprinkle over the top the ¼ cup brown sugar. Bake 50-60 minutes at 325°. Serve with whipped cream.

Rhubarb Betty

5 cups rhubarb, cut in 1" pieces, or 2 pkgs. frozen rhubarb
¼ cup butter
6 slices whole wheat bread, cubed with crusts removed
1 cup brown sugar
1 tsp. cinnamon

Turn oven to 375°. Grease 1½-quart casserole. Melt butter and mix thoroughly with bread cubes. Arrange alternate layers of bread cubes and rhubarb in casserole. Sprinkle each layer of fruit with sugar and cinnamon. When using frozen rhubarb, reduce sugar to ½ cup. Finish with a layer of bread cubes. Cover and bake 35 minutes. Uncover and bake 15 minutes longer. Serve warm with cream. Serves 4-6.

Steamed Carrot Pudding

1 cup *sifted* whole wheat flour
½ tsp. cloves
½ tsp. nutmeg
1 tsp. cinnamon
½ tsp. soda
2 tsp. baking powder
½ cup butter
½ cup raw or brown sugar
½ cup molasses
1 cup grated raw carrots
1 cup grated raw potatoes
1 cup grated raw apples
1 cup raisins
½ cup nuts (optional)

Sift together, twice, the flour, soda, baking powder and spices. Cream butter and sugar. Add molasses. Combine all ingredients and steam in greased mold 2-3 hours. Serve hot with lemon or vanilla sauce.

DESSERTS

Lemon or Vanilla Sauce

¾ cup raw or brown sugar
3 tbsp. cornstarch
¼ tsp. salt
¼ tsp. nutmeg
2 cups boiling water
2 tbsp. butter
3 tbsp. lemon juice or
1 tsp. vanilla

Combine sugar, cornstarch, salt and nutmeg. Gradually add hot water and cook over low heat or in double boiler until thick and clear. Add butter and lemon juice (or vanilla) and blend.

Steamed Holiday Pudding

1 cup *sifted* whole wheat flour
¼ tsp. salt
1 tsp. soda
1 tsp. nutmeg
1 tsp. cinnamon
1 cup whole wheat bread crumbs
1 cup milk
⅓ cup oil
¾ cup raw or brown sugar
2 eggs, beaten
½ cup nuts
1 cup seedless raisins

Sift together, twice, the flour, salt, soda, and spices. Soak bread crumbs in milk. Combine oil, sugar and beaten eggs and add to crumb mixture. Add dry ingredients. Stir in nuts and raisins. Fill pudding molds ⅔ full and steam 2 hours. Serve with lemon or vanilla sauce and whipped cream.

Steamed Carrot Pudding (with Suet)

1 cup *sifted* whole wheat flour
½ tsp. soda
1 tsp. baking powder
½ tsp. nutmeg
½ tsp. cloves
½ tsp. cinnamon
½ cup whole wheat bread crumbs
1 cup ground raw carrots
1 cup ground raw apples (unpeeled)
1 cup ground suet
1 cup seedless raisins
½ cup raw or brown sugar
½ cup molasses
1 egg, beaten
½ cup nuts (optional)

Sift dry ingredients together twice. Combine all ingredients. Place in greased molds and steam 3 hours. This pudding is delicious served with vanilla ice cream or with a lemon sauce and whipped cream or with Hard Sauce.

Note: When buying suet, have the butcher grind it for you. It can be stored indefinitely in the refrigerator in a bottle or other container with a good lid.

DESSERTS

Steamed Sago Pudding

⅓ cup sago,* washed 3 or 4 times
3 cups milk
3 cups dry whole wheat bread crumbs
6 tbsp. butter or margarine
1½ cups brown or raw sugar
1 tsp. soda, dissolved in 2 tbsp. milk
3 tsp. baking powder
1 cup chopped nuts (optional)
3 cups raisins or currants, or
　1½ cups of each

*Medium-size tapioca, not instant, can be used.

Soak sago in 3 cups milk overnight. Combine all ingredients and stir well. Steam for 2½ hours in pudding molds or double boiler (⅔ full). Two no. 2 size cans may be used for molds. Serve with custard sauce, or lemon or vanilla sauce and/or whipped cream. Serves about 15.

Economical Bread Pudding

2 cups milk
2 tbsp. butter
1 cup soft whole wheat bread crumbs
　(day-old with crust removed)
6 tbsp. raw or brown sugar
¼ tsp. salt
2 eggs, beaten
1 tsp. vanilla
dash of nutmeg

Scald milk and butter. Add crumbs, sugar and salt and let soak a few minutes. Stir in eggs and vanilla. Pour into 1-quart baking dish. Set in pan of hot water and bake 40 minutes at 375°. Serves 6-8.

Variation: Add ¼ cup coconut.

Real English Plum Pudding

½ lb. finely chopped suet
½ lb. raisins, seedless
½ lb. currants
½ lb. white raisins (golden)
½ lb. chopped, mixed peel
½ lb. dried plums, if available
1½ cups *sifted* whole wheat flour
½ tsp. allspice
½ tsp. cinnamon
½ tsp. nutmeg
¼ tsp. cloves
¼ tsp. ginger
¼ tsp. mace
½ tsp. salt
1 tsp. baking powder
1½ cups whole wheat bread crumbs
1½ cups brown sugar
4 eggs, well beaten
½ cup molasses
¼ cup apricot nectar or other fruit juice
½ cup chopped nuts

Combine suet and prepared fruit. Sift in a little of the flour, and toss to blend. Sift remaining flour with spices, baking powder and salt. Stir into fruit along with bread crumbs and brown sugar. Beat eggs thoroughly and combine with molasses and fruit juice. Stir into fruit and flour mixture until well blended. Add nuts.

Spoon batter into two 1-quart molds, or the equivalent, which have been well greased. Cover molds with double thickness of foil. Set them on a rack in large kettle. Add boiling water halfway up the side. Cover kettle and steam 3 hours after water comes to a boil again. Serve hot with desired sauce. Serves 15.

This pudding may be made weeks in advance and stored in a cool place, or frozen. Reheat thoroughly by steaming for at least 1 hour.

DESSERTS

Steamed Banana Pudding

2 tbsp. granulated sugar
6 tbsp. water
3 cups *sifted* whole wheat flour
4 tsp. baking powder
½ tsp. salt
¾ cup butter or margarine
1½ cups light brown sugar
1 tsp. vanilla
3 eggs, beaten
2 large bananas, mashed
1 cup milk
1 cup chopped nuts (optional)

Caramelize the 2 tbsp. sugar in frying pan and add the 6 tbsp. water to liquefy. Sift together, twice, the flour, baking powder and salt. Cream butter and sugar and add vanilla and liquefied caramelized sugar. Add eggs and beat. Blend in mashed bananas. Add dry ingredients alternately with milk. Add nuts. Pour into three 1-quart buttered pudding molds (3 no. 2½-size cans) and steam two hours. Serve with custard sauce or whipped cream.

Note: Jello vanilla pudding may be used for the custard sauce.

Cracked Wheat Pudding

(This is a tasty way to use leftover cracked wheat cereal.)

3 eggs, beaten
3 cups milk
1 cup seedless raisins
2 cups cooked cracked wheat cereal (salted)
¼ cup honey
2 tsp. grated orange rind
¼ tsp. mace
⅛ tsp. salt

Combine all ingredients in a large bowl. Pour into well-buttered 2-qt. casserole and bake 1 hour at 325°-350°. Serve hot or cold, topped with cream and sliced fresh fruit, lightly sweetened with honey.

Lemon Dessert

2 tbsp. butter or margarine
⅔ cup raw or brown sugar
2 eggs, separated
3 tbsp. whole wheat flour
pinch of salt
juice of 1 lemon
½ tsp. grated lemon rind
1 cup milk

Cream butter and sugar, add beaten egg yolks, whole wheat flour, salt and lemon juice. Mix thoroughly. Add milk. Fold in stiffly beaten egg whites. Pour into buttered casserole and bake in pan of water 35 minutes at 325°-350°.

DESSERTS

Cream Puffs

½ cup butter or margarine
1 cup water
1 cup *unsifted* whole wheat flour
4 eggs

Bring butter and water to a boil. Turn off heat. Add flour all at once. Stir vigorously until mixture leaves sides of pan and forms a ball. Remove from stove. Add eggs, one at a time, beating well after each addition. Spoon balls of dough onto ungreased baking sheet, making 12 large or 16 medium-sized puffs. Bake 1 hour at 350°-375°, or until bubbles of moisture disappear from shells. When cold, cut a slit in the side and spoon in favorite filling (recipe below) or whipped cream.

Cream Puff Filling

2 cups milk
¾ cup raw or brown sugar
5½ tbsp. whole wheat flour
⅛ tsp. salt
2 eggs, beaten
1 tsp. vanilla
1 cup whipping cream

Scald milk. Mix sugar, flour and salt and add to hot milk. Stir constantly over low heat until thickened and smooth. Cook over hot water in double boiler for 15 minutes. Gradually add cooked mixture to beaten eggs. Return to double boiler and cook 3-4 minutes, stirring constantly. Chill. Fold in whipped cream and vanilla.

Jelly Roll

4 eggs
1 tsp. baking powder
¼ tsp. salt
¾ cup raw or brown sugar
1 tsp. vanilla
¾ cup *sifted* whole wheat flour
1 cup jelly

Combine eggs, baking powder and salt in large bowl of mixer. Beat, adding sugar gradually, until mixture becomes thick and fluffy. Fold in vanilla and flour. Turn into 8" x 12" pan which has been greased, lined with paper to within ½" of edge and the paper again greased. Bake 13-15 minutes at 350°-375°. While cake is still in pan quickly cut off crisp edges.

Turn out onto a damp cloth. Remove paper. Spread with jelly or jam and roll from long side at once. Wrap in cloth and cool on rack.

DESSERTS

General Suggestions on Pie Crust

We highly recommend that when making pastry you use *whole wheat pastry flour*. This may be obtained in health food stores.

For greater nutrition, add ¼ cup wheat germ for each crust. It does not detract from tenderness and gives a rich, nutty flavor. Watch closely when baking, as it burns easily. Reduce heat if necessary.

Do not stir, knead, or handle dough any more than is absolutely necessary.

Roll out on a lightly floured canvas-covered board with a rolling pin covered with a knitted stocking. These materials hold flour and prevent dough from sticking.

Crusts made with oil can be delicious and crisp, but never flaky.

Flaky Pie Crust

1. Fat must be chilled. Natural lard (not hydrogenated) makes the flakiest crust. Chilled margarine or chilled butter may also be used satisfactorily.
2. Cut fat into flour only until the pieces are the size of large peas.
3. Water used should be "ice water."
4. Bake at high temperatures—425° for 8-10 minutes. This temperature is necessary so the crust will bake before the fat has a chance to melt and penetrate evenly throughout the flour. Flakiness results because the dough and fat are still in layers. To obtain still better results, chill or freeze crust before baking.

Flaky Pie Crust (two 9" crusts)

1½ cups *sifted* whole wheat flour (whole wheat pastry flour preferred)
1 tsp. salt (scant)

Sift together twice and place in mixing bowl.

Add:

½ cup wheat germ (untoasted)
½ cup lard or ⅔ cup thoroughly chilled margarine or butter

Cut shortening into dry ingredients with pastry cutter or two knives until particles of fat are the size of large peas.

Add:

¼ cup *ice water*

Mix only enough to moisten ingredients. Turn dough onto a canvas-covered, floured board. Divide into two parts. Pat dough quickly into a flat round ball; dust lightly with flour, and roll ⅛" thick. Use a circular motion with the rolling pin to make a perfect circle. Avoid handling dough. Turn canvas if necessary.

Turn pie tin over dough. Lift canvas and dough over tin and remove canvas. Trim and flute edges. Perforate with fork if for a single crust, at ½" intervals. Chill or freeze if time permits. Or add filling and top crust. Bake in preheated 425° oven 8-10 minutes for single crust. For double-crust pies, bake 8-10 minutes, then reduce temperature to 325° for 30-35 minutes for uncooked fruit pies, or 20 minutes for mincemeat or canned fruit fillings.

DESSERTS

Crisp Pie Crust (Never Flaky)

2 cups *sifted* whole flour (pastry flour preferred)
¾ tsp. salt
Sift together twice.
Beat with fork to combine:
½ cup oil
¼ cup ice water

Blend liquid into flour with fork. Form into ball. Proceed as for Flaky Pie Crust. Bake 15-18 minutes at 350°.

Egg-Vinegar Pie Crust

2½ cups *sifted* whole wheat flour
1 cup chilled lard, margarine or butter
1 tsp. salt
1 egg
1 tbsp. vinegar
6-8 tbsp. ice water

Cut fat into flour and salt, which have been sifted together twice, until "large pea" consistency. With a fork, combine beaten egg, vinegar and ice water. Blend together all ingredients with a fork. Divide into three balls. Roll out thin. Makes 3 8" pie shells. Bake 8-10 minutes at 425°.

Graham Cracker-Wheat Germ Pie Crust

Blend together:

½ cup wheat germ
¾ cup crushed graham crackers
  or dry cake crumbs (see Wheatnuts
  recipe in Cereal Section)
⅓ cup melted butter
1 tbsp. honey

Press into an 8" or 9" pie tin. Chill and fill with your favorite filling.

Variation:

Substitute ⅔ cup whole wheat bread crumbs for cracker crumbs. Reduce wheat germ to ¼ cup and add ¼ cup powdered milk and ½ tsp. cinnamon.

RECIPES

Cereals

Whole Wheat (Steamed) 38
Whole Wheat
  (Oven Cooked) 38
Whole Wheat (Crockpot) 39
Whole Wheat (Thermos) 39
Canned Wheat 39
Cracked Wheat Cereal 40
Cracked Wheat
  (Crockpot) 40
Gruel 41
Whole Wheat Flour Cereal 41
Toasted Wheat Germ 42
Chewy Cold Cereal 42
Wheatnuts 43
Granola Cereal 44
Bulgur Wheat 44

Breads and Rolls—Yeast

General Bread-Making
  Suggestions 48
Molding a Perfect Loaf
  of Bread 51
Superior, Quick Whole
  Wheat Bread 52
Spoon Bread 53
Buttermilk Bread 53
Basic Whole Wheat Bread 54
Honey-Oatmeal Bread 56
No-Knead Raisin Bread 57
Orange-Currant Loaf 57
Quick Two-Hour
  Buttercrust Bread 58
Easy Raisin Buns 58
Dilly Casserole Bread 59
Herb Batter Bread 60
Whole Wheat
  French Bread 61
It's All in the Way
  You Roll the Roll 62
  Parker House Rolls
  Cloverleaf Rolls
  Hamburger Rolls
  Hot Dog Rolls
  Butterflake Rolls
  Crescents
  Sweet Rolls
  Muffins
Special Dinner Party Rolls 63
Refrigerator Rolls 64
Quick Orange Glaze 65
Basic Sweet Dough 65
Cinnamon Rolls 66
Cinnamon Roll Topping 66
Swedish Tea Ring 67
Filled Sweet Dough Ring 67
Orange Rolls 68
Bohemian Bread 68
Danish Coffee Twist 69
Honey Glaze 69
Russian Holiday Bread 70
No-Knead Potato Refrigerator
  Rolls 70
German Stollen 71
Russian Sweet Bread 72
Braided Sweet Bread 73
Yeast Corn Bread 74
Yeast Raised Doughnuts 75
Sesame Buns 76
Yeast Waffles 77
Pancakes 77

Bread and Rolls—Quick

Orange Bread 80
Apple Loaf 80
Applesauce-Banana Bread 81
Canadian Banana Bread 81
Orange Marmalade
  Quick Bread 82
Nut Bread 82
Prune Bread 83
Date-Nut Bread 83
Oatmeal Spice Bread 84
Deluxe Hot Cakes 84
Spiced Applesauce-Currant
  Loaf 85
Dried Apricot Bread 85
Date-Nut Orange Bread 86
Corn Bread 86
Boston Brown Bread 87
Muffins 87
Steamed Honey-Date
  or Honey-Raisin Bread 88
Baking Powder Biscuits 88
Six-Week Bran Muffins 89
All-Bran Muffins 89
Baking Powder
  Cinnamon Rolls 90
French Toast 90
Irish Soda Scone 91
Waffles 91
Breakfast Sweet Bread 92
Wheatquick Mix No. 1 92
Wheatquick Mix No. 2 93

Meats, Casseroles

Gluten 96

RECIPES

Seasoned Flour   99
Casserole Steak   99
Cubed Steak   99
Beef Short Ribs   100
Stuffed Lamb or
   Pork Chops   100
Roasted Meat   101
Swiss Steak   101
Spoon-Burgers
   (Sloppy-Joes)   102
Hamburgers   102
Hamburger Gravy   102
Hamburger Meatballs   103
Danish Frikadeller
   (Beef Patties)   103
Hamburgers with
   Barbecue Sauce   103
Barbecue Sauce   103
Swiss Meatballs   105
Hamburger Roll-Ups   105
Tri-Meat Loaf   106
Meat Loaf   106
Hamburger Stroganoff   107
Stuffed Meat Loaf   108
Spanish Wheat   108
Angela's Dutch
   Meat Loaf   109

Hamburger Cracked
   Wheat Casserole   110
Chinese Noodle Casserole   110
Brown Beef Stew   111
Glorified Stew   112
Lamb's Fry (Liver)   113
Liver Patties   114
Easy Chicken Casserole   115
Chicken Paprika   116
Delicious Well-Done
   Chicken   116
Poultry Dressing   117
Poultry Stuffing (Moist)   117
Poultry Stuffing (Dry)   118
French Harvest
   Chicken Casserole   118
Chicken Pie   119
Baked Chicken Squares   120
Chicken-Mushroom
   Sauce   120
Fish   121
Fillet of Fish   121
Salmon Loaf   122
Sea Food Casserole   122
Stuffed Halibut Steaks   123
Tuna Fish Loaf with
   Celery-Olive Sauce   124

Economical Ham Loaf   124
Tuna Fish Roll-Ups   125
Tamale Pie   126
Beef and Potato Casserole   127
Corned Beef Casserole   127
Corned Beef Loaf   128
Armenian Cabbage Rolls   128
Crab Casserole   129
Onion-Wheat Casserole   129
Asparagus and
   Ham au Gratin   130
Cracked Wheat-Lentil
   Casserole   131
Italian Macaroni Loaf   132
Mushroom Sauce   132

Vegetables

Western Celery Casserole   134
Asparagus and Egg
   Casserole   134
Dutch Snap Beans   135
Cabbage Timbale   135
Baked Corn and
   Tomatoes   136
Scalloped Tomatoes   136
Scalloped Corn   137

Zucchini Squash
   Casserole   137
Potatoes au Gratin   138
Baked Zucchini Squash
   (Stuffed)   138

Soups, Sauces, Savories

White Sauces   140
Feather Dumplings   141
Whole Wheat Herb
   Dumplings   142
Whole Wheat Batter
   (Croquettes or Patties)   142
Salad Croutons   143
Economical Potato Soup   143
Baked Omelet   144
Ham and Cheese Fondue   144
Split Pea Soup   145
Danish Soup   146
Chili Beef on Buns   147
Nourishing Sandwich
   Filling   147
Hot Tuna Sandwich   148

Cookies

Refrigerator Cookies   150

RECIPES

Oatmeal Refrigerator Cookies 150
Date Pinwheel Cookies 151
Date-Nut Refrigerator Cookies 152
Orange Roll-Out Cookies 152
Rolled Sugar Cookies (Key Recipe) 153
Cinnamon Pecan Bars 153
Filled Sugar Cookies 153
Peanut Butter Cookies 154
Thumb Print Cookies 154
Sour Cream Cookies 155
Raisin-Filled Cookies 156
Snickerdoodle Cookies 157
Crisp Gingersnaps 157
Crunchy Cookies 158
Soft Molasses Ginger Cookies 158
Oatmeal Cookies 159
Raisin Drop Cookies 159
Carrot Cookies (Cooked Carrots) 160
Carrot Cookies (Raw Carrots) 160
Applesauce Cookies 161
Whole Wheat Macaroons 161
Butterscotch Cookies 162
Brown-Butter Icing 162
Drop Sugar Cookies 163
Pineapple Cookies 163
Banana-Oatmeal Cookies 164
Coconut Drop Cookies 164
Pineapple Squares 165
Raw Apple Cookies 166
Caramel Nut Squares 167
Carob Brownies 168
Prize-Winning Brownies 168
Date-Nut Bars 169
Butterscotch Picnic Bars 169
Raisin-Nut Squares (Bars) 170
Spicy Drop Cookies 170
Honey-Date Bars 171
Filled Cupcakes 171
Coconut-Nut Cookies 172
Yule Cookies 173
Jumbo Raisin Cookies 174

Cakes

General Suggestions 176
Perfect Plain Whole Wheat Cake 177
Orange-Whipped Cream Sauce 178
Pineapple Filling 178
Spicy Peach Sauce 178
Whipped Banana Topping 179
Thrifty Pineapple Topping or Filling 179
Crunchy Topping 180
Spice Cake 180
Divinity Frosting 181
Broiled Coconut Icing 181
Coconut Cake 181
Never-Fail Sheet Cake with Topping 182
Maple Seafoam Frosting 183
Soft Gingerbread 183
Prize Sponge Cake 184
Chiffon Cake 185
Date Cake 186
Prune Cake 187
Carob Frosting 187
Chocolate Sour Cream Cake 188
Pineapple Upside-Down Cake 189
Banana-Nut Loaf Cake 190
Economy (Eggless) Cake 190
Shortcake 191
Boiled Raisin Cake 192
Ground-Raisin Cake 193
Seven-Minute Icing 193
Applesauce Cake 194
Fruit Cake 195
German Apple Streusel Cake 196
Dutch Hustle Cake 197
Peach Crumbly Cake 198
New Zealand Apple Shortcake 199
Swiss Spiced Carrot Cake 199
Pineapple Breakfast Cake 200
Pineapple Topping 200
Oatmeal Cake with Broiled Topping 201
Broiled Topping 201
Alternate Quick Topping 201
Butterscotch Morsel Cake 202
Raisin Cupcakes 302
Butterscotch Cream Icing 203
Orange-Date Cake 204
Orange Kiss-Me Cake 205

Desserts

Canadian Apple
　Dumplings   208
Apple Crunch Supreme   209
Caramel Sauce   209
Best-Ever Apple Pudding   210
Fruit Crisp (Key Recipe)   211
Fruit Cobbler
　(Key Recipe)   211
Date Pudding   212
Mystery Pudding   212
Rhubarb Betty   213
Steamed Carrot Pudding   213
Lemon or Vanilla Sauce   214
Steamed Holiday
　Pudding   214
Steamed Carrot Pudding
　(with Suet)   215
Steamed Sago Pudding   216
Economical Bread
　Pudding   216
Real English Plum
　Pudding   217
Steamed Banana Bread   218
Cracked Wheat Pudding   219
Lemon Dessert   219
Cream Puffs   220
Cream Puff Filling   220
Jelly Roll   221
General Suggestions on
　Pie Crust   222
Flaky Pie Crust
　Suggestions   222
Flaky Pie Crust Recipe   223
Crisp Pie Crust   224
Egg-Vinegar Pie Crust   224
Graham Cracker-Wheat Germ
　Pie Crust   225